AROUND PRESTON

Copyright © David John Hindle 2012

Published by Palatine Books
an imprint of Carnegie Publishing Ltd
Carnegie House
Chatsworth Road
Lancaster
LA1 4SL
www.carnegiepublishing.com

ISBN: 978-1-874181-92-7

Designed and typeset by Carnegie Book Production, Lancaster
Printed and bound in the UK by Page Bros Ltd, Norwich

AROUND PRESTON

Heritage, Natural History & Walking
in the City & Beautiful Countryside Beyond

DAVID JOHN HINDLE M.A.

Contents

Foreword

On February 27, 1836, readers of the *Preston Chronicle* opened its pages to discover an article on the 'gratifying changes' taking place in Preston. The Green Bank Estate, extending northward from Moor Lane and Fylde Street to Moor Park Brook, 'which has long been occupied as gardens and small fields and forms an airy and salubrious eminence rising towards the middle, will, probably in a year or two, become a sort of new town, or compact manufacturing district, and the neatness and convenience of the houses will, we doubt not, render it the favourite residence of a large portion of our operative community, for whom it is principally intended.' The article continued that 'the supply of water afforded by the brook, as well as by springs and streamlets on each side, together with other local advantages, render this valley a peculiarly suitable site for a considerable number of cotton works.' It was a moment of realisation that the industrial despoliation of the natural landscape was a price that had to be paid for being a leading manufacturing town in nineteenth-century Britain. Some 200 years later, a new age has dawned, the satanic cotton mills with their smoking chimney stacks are gone, and nature, albeit precariously, is returning to sites once blighted by the advance of industry.

This timely book, written by David Hindle to commemorate Preston Guild 2012, takes us on a series of heritage and natural-history walks in Preston and its wider surroundings, highlighting places of historic interest, the flora, fauna and, in particular, the ornithology of the region. David, who is president of Preston Historical Society, is a rare combination of broadcaster, naturalist and local historian. He is one of the authors of the standard work on Lancashire ornithology, *The Birds of Lancashire*, and indeed nine other books on local and natural history. David Hindle is a tireless campaigner for the preservation of wildlife and what is left of our unspoilt countryside was once described by Hubert Parry as 'England's green and pleasant land.' In the context of conservation one of the walks included here features

Opposite Grimsargh Reservoir at daybreak. *Courtesy of Nellie Carbis.*

Grimsargh wetlands, an important local nature reserve comprising three redundant reservoirs, which is of regional significance for its flora, breeding birds and other wildlife. It was at the author's instigation that this site was awarded Biological Heritage Site status in August 2003. Another walk, *Walking in the Footsteps of Cromwell*, describes the Battle of Preston that took place on August 17, 1648, and takes us past Red Scar Wood, which covers a precipitate incline on the banks of the Ribble.

Red Scar was recognised as a scene of unrivalled beauty by an earlier local historian, Charles Hardwick, who published his *History of the Borough of Preston and its Environs* in 1857. It is not generally known that Hardwick was also a skilful amateur artist. Describing how the trees 'cling tenaciously to the crumbling earth', he adds that 'the subject is not quite wild and savage enough for the pencil of Salvator Rosa'. Such a comparison of Red Scar Wood with 'Savage' Rosa (a seventeenth-century Italian landscape painter known for his wild and rugged scenes) would have come more easily from an eighteenth-century tourist to the lakes in search of the picturesque, rather than from a Victorian local historian!

Readers following this absorbing Ribble Valley walk from Walton-le-Dale to Grimsargh may wish to take a short detour along the Red Scar Memorial Walk, also founded by the author in 2004, which takes in the history of the former Red Scar mansion and its association with the Cross family. Further details of this short circular walk beginning at Preston Crematorium may be obtained from a splendid interpretive board situated alongside the Guild Wheel, and from a specially prepared leaflet which may be obtained at the Cemetery Office or Preston Visitor Information Centre.

David's dedication to his subject can be seen in the wide variety of walks, which take us from Preston to Hoghton Tower, Clitheroe and the Bleasdale Circle, among many other locations. Furthermore it is his ability to combine his knowledge of the natural environment with local history which makes his book all the more engaging. But his interest in his subject is not confined to the past. New threats to the natural heritage present themselves today; wildlife can be damaged by scientific methods employed for greater efficiency in modern agriculture; and sometimes well-intentioned heritage schemes which allow for greater public access can intrude on the very landscapes they have been designed to protect. If David Hindle's book can serve to encourage a greater respect for our natural environment, then it will have been worthwhile for the sake of future generations.

Stephen Sartin
August 2012

Introduction

This book aims to celebrate certain aspects of the history and natural history of the region by exploring Preston and the beautiful countryside surrounding the city, including the unspoilt river Ribble and its tributaries. My own observations have been carried out in this area over many years. The Ribble and Hodder valleys in particular are two of the most picturesque in England, nestling in a landscape moulded by the last ice age and encompassing some of the most interesting buildings and historic sites in Lancashire. I personally think that birds live in the nicest of places and one does not have to travel far from Preston to discover that in many instances birds also live in areas that are steeped in fascinating history, and thus the two interests are compatible and complement each other. Here are new treasures just waiting to be discovered by everyone, including those visiting Preston for the first time during guild year.

All encounters with every aspect of the natural world have, for as long as I remember, appealed to my senses. The Forest of Bowland Area of Outstanding Natural Beauty (AONB) is always well worth a visit; on a beautiful, frosty winter's day the pristine ancient landscape looks magnificent and a camera is recommended to capture memorable moments. It is even on record that when her Majesty the Queen visited the county in her role as Duke of Lancaster, she said that if she was ever allowed to retire, it would be to the Ribble Valley, in the heart of Lancashire. What better recommendation than a royal seal of approval for the breathtaking landscapes skirting the Forest of Bowland and its quaint villages at the core of the Duchy of Lancaster. These carefully selected walks are ideal for those who wish to escape either alone or with their friends and families to areas off the beaten track. The use of public transport provides a greater freedom to complete linear walks and most of the walks are served by local bus services that even penetrate Bowland via Whitewell and the Hodder Valley to Slaidburn and beyond. All walks are easy unless stated otherwise. Directions, approximate distances, and duration are also shown, though you are strongly advised to use the relevant Ordnance Survey maps – *Outdoor Leisure No. 41, Forest of Bowland* and *Sheet 102, Landranger Series*

Her Majesty the Queen at Dunsop Bridge. *Author's collection.*

– and to remember that when birdwatching a good pair of binoculars and a reliable birdwatching book are both essential. I started off with the well-known *Observer's Book of Birds* which has now been superseded by a vast range of ornithological guides and literature that have flooded the market in recent years. Understanding the specific habitat requirements of individual species is crucial when birdwatching, especially for anyone wanting to take their birdwatching to a more advanced level, and keeping a record of all that you see is one of the hallmarks of being a good birder.

Throughout the described heritage and natural history walks, birds are the real attraction because they are so obvious, though sadly many of the 246 breeding species in Britain are in serious trouble, although a smaller percentage are expanding their range, such as the buzzard, little egret, avocet and great spotted woodpecker. Priority species in need of conservation include farmland and woodland birds, seabirds and many summer migrants. For example, skylarks were until recently a leading contender to be seen and heard over farmland but nowadays are in steep decline and almost a thing of the past, not just in many parts of Lancashire but indeed throughout much of the UK. Conservation is science-based and it is the science that provides the evidence to drive forward the frontiers of human knowledge in order to protect the environment and habitat and to examine how diminishing populations of our impoverished wildlife might be reversed.

So, why not make the most of what there is to see and discover Preston and the surrounding countryside during guild year? Enjoy all of the walks, set your own pace, whilst taking time to watch and reflect. You can also revel in the fact that walking is an excellent way of keeping mentally and physically fit, and may even enrich the soul and perhaps provide a stimulus for further interest and research.

'Take 5' – a group of cyclists enjoying the panoramic view of the Vale of Chipping from Jeffrey Fell. *Courtesy of Graham Wilkinson.*

Acknowledgements

Once again it is a pleasure to acknowledge the help given by the following people and organisations in the production of this book. Anna Goddard and Alistair Hodge at Carnegie Publishing for their expertise and patience; Dr Malcolm Greenhalgh, Stan Owen, the late Nellie Carbis, Peter Smith, Norman Duerden, Phil Garlington, David Prowse and Graham Wilkinson for supplying excellent photographs and artwork; Dr Alan Crosby for reading and commenting on the history content; the staff at the Lancashire Archives and the Harris Library, Preston; and acclaimed Preston historian Stephen Sartin for writing the foreword and finally my wife Dorothy for her overall support.

Disclaimer

The author has walked and researched the routes for the purpose of this guide. Whilst every effort has been made to represent the routes accurately, all distances are approximate and neither the author nor the publisher can accept any responsibility in connection with any trespass, loss or injury arising from the use of the definitive route or any associated route. Changes may occur in the landscape, which may affect the information in this book and the author and publisher would welcome notification of any such changes. That said, we sincerely hope that the walks provide many hours of enjoyment.

Information

For full details of passenger services on the Ribble Steam visit the website www.ribblesteam.org.uk or telephone 01772 728800.
For more information about bus routes visit the website www.traveline.info or telephone Traveline (bus enquiries) on 0871 200 22 33.

Opposite Winter wonderland – the river Ribble at Red Scar. *Author's collection.*

Further Reading

Birds of Lancashire and North Merseyside, Jones, Hindle, Walsh, White et al., 2007, Hobby Publications
Birds of Lancashire, Oakes, 1953, Oliver & Boyd
Ribble: River and Valley, Greenhalgh, 2009, Carnegie Publishing
Birdwatching Walks in Bowland, Hindle and Wilson, 2005, Palatine Books
Birdwatching Walks around Morecambe Bay, Hindle and Wilson, 2007, Palatine Books
All Stations to Longridge, Hindle, 2010, Amberley Publishing
Grimsargh: the Story of a Lancashire Village, Hindle, 2002, Carnegie Publishing
Victorian Preston and the Whittingham Hospital Railway, Hindle, 2012, Amberley Publishing
A History of Preston, Hewitson, 1883, EP Publishing
The People and Places of Historic Preston, Sartin, 1988, Carnegie Publishing
History of Preston, Hunt, 2009, Carnegie Publishing

'Proud Preston'

In Commemoration of Preston's Famous Guild

Before moving on to the walks we begin with a brief introduction to the history of Preston. Preston (a city since 2002) is especially famous for its Guild Merchant conferred by ancient charter in 1179 by Henry II. 'Once every Preston Guild' is a local expression meaning not very often, and a reference to the fact that the celebrations happen every twenty years – although it was only after 1542 that the twenty-year cycle was adopted. The sequence of guilds has only been interrupted once, because of wartime hostilities in 1942, and it was not until September 1952, that the guild mayor, Alderman John James Ward, restored the guild celebrations at the much-lamented old Public Hall. The Guild Merchant originally allowed time for the burgesses to confirm their rights, revise statutes and to register their sons on the guild rolls, a legal function known as the 'Orders of the Guild'. By the end of the eighteenth century the formalities and legalistic aspects associated with the ancient guild institution were evolving into a popular festival. The guild of 1802 witnessed the rise of free trade and a definite festival atmosphere which superseded the more formal proceedings of the past when the burgesses held the monopoly of the town's trade.

During the eighteenth century, 'Proud Preston' changed from being a haven for fashionable society to a hot bed of workers labouring in the cotton and engineering industries. When Daniel Defoe visited Preston in 1724 he described the town as he saw it: 'Preston is a fine town, and tolerably full of people, but not like Liverpool or Manchester; besides, we come now beyond the trading part of the county. Here is no manufacture; the town is full of attorneys, proctors and notaries.' By the time of the Industrial Revolution the town's first cotton-spinning mill had opened on Moor Lane in 1777. Preston was at the forefront of automation when John Horrocks opened

Opposite Preston Guild 1972 – the Trades Procession in Friargate. *Author's collection.*

At the beginning of the nineteenth century, attorneys, businessmen and the gentlemen of Preston moved out to rural areas. One example was William Cross who took up residence at Red Scar at Grimsargh-with-Brockholes. *Red Scar mansion, watercolour by Albert Woods.*

his first factory in 1790, closely followed by three more factories during the same decade. This was due in no small measure due to one of Preston's most famous sons, Sir Richard Arkwright. Born in 1732, Arkwright became a barber and wig maker residing in Back Lane, off Friargate, in what is now known as 'Arkwright House' at the rear of the parish church, the scene of his greatest invention in 1768. Arising from his expertise as a wig maker he developed and patented a water-frame-based spinning machine that was to be a catalyst for the mechanisation of the industry throughout Britain, eventually superseding the small-scale handloom weaving industry.

The textile industry helped create a new urban industrialised working class and a six-fold increase in the population of Preston during the first half of the nineteenth century, rising from 11,887 in 1801 to 69,542 in 1851.

During the latter half of the nineteenth century the high rate of population growth abated and the social conditions in the town improved, with less overcrowding, higher wages and a better standard of living for a population of 112,989 by 1901. Preston was transformed into a town crammed with mills, terraced houses and cobbled streets, when at the height of the Industrial Revolution 'King Cotton' reigned supreme.

Charles Dickens visited Preston in 1853 and is said to have gained some inspiration for his description of Coketown in *Hard Times*. The following extract from the book paints a vivid picture of a town in Victorian England and describes the prevailing social conditions, the New Church (likened to Preston's present minster), religious persuasions and the influence of the Temperance Movement at the height of the Industrial Revolution.

> Coketown was a town of red brick, or of brick that would have been red if the smoke and ashes had allowed it; but as matters stood it was a town of unnatural red and black like the painted face of a savage. It was a town of machinery and tall chimneys, out of which interminable serpents of smoke trailed them for ever and ever and never got uncoiled. It had a black canal in it, and a river that ran purple with ill-smelling dye, and vast piles of buildings full of windows where there was a rattling and a trembling all day long, and where the piston of the steam-engine worked monotonously up and down like the head of an elephant in a state of melancholy madness. It contained several large streets all very like one another, and many small streets still more like one another, inhabited by people equally like one another, who all went in and out at the same hours, with the same sound upon the same pavements, to do the same work, and to whom every day was the same as yesterday and tomorrow, and every year the counterpart of the last and the next ... The jail might have been the infirmary, the infirmary might have been the jail, the town hall might have been either or both ... You saw nothing in Coketown but what was severely workful ... If the members of a religious persuasion built a chapel there – as the members of eighteen religious persuasions had done – they made it a pious warehouse of red brick, with sometimes a bell in a birdcage on the top of it. The solitary exception was the New Church, a stuccoed edifice with a square steeple over the door, terminating in four short pinnacles like florid wooden legs. Then came the Teetotal Society, who complained that these same people would get drunk, and showed in tabular statements that they did get drunk, and proved that no inducement, human or Divine (except a medal), would induce them to forego their custom of getting drunk.

This extract of Dickens' work encapsulates well the image of Preston, as a Victorian northern mill town. Well-documented sources elsewhere reflect the level of abject poverty, appalling housing conditions, disease and high infant mortality at the time of his visits. On a brighter note and alluding to 'Proud Preston', Victorian historian and journalist Anthony Hewitson quotes historian James Ray when describing the town in 1758: 'Preston is one of the prettiest retirements in England, the resort of beautiful and agreeable ladies and a large number of gentry, which was unexcelled for the politeness of its inhabitants, and vulgarly called 'Proud Preston' on account of its being a place of the best fashion.' Hewitson also refers to the very real advances made by the time of the 1882 Preston Guild in the social and physical fabric of the town.

Preston has long been at the hub of the road and rail network, and is the administrative centre of Lancashire County Council. Preston Railway Station was rebuilt in 1880 at a cost of £200,000 to replace the primitive North Union Station of 1838, and the foundation stone was laid for Preston Dock in 1885, replacing the earlier Port of Preston established in 1843 on the banks of the Ribble.

As a Prestonian born and bred, with ancestral roots in the town, and having witnessed the guilds of 1952, 1972, 1992 and Preston Guild 2012, I remain confident that our historic city will long be recognised as 'Proud Preston'.

A view of Preston past

What follows is a wonderful contemporary account of 1881, one year before the guild of 1882. It is altogether a fascinating insight into Victorian Preston and a significant source of primary material sourced from a contemporay journal published in 1881.

Fishergate stretches out bravely before us, with bonnet-shops, booksellers, 'and bootmakers, side by side with the palatial Preston Banking Company's premises—a costly, lofty, highly decorated, three-storied, Italian building— dwarfing its unpretending neighbours the chandler's, chemist's, hairdresser's, tailor's, and butcher's shops. Then the Preston Pilot office, in Clarke's stationer's shop; another stationer's at the side of it; and the Lancaster Banking Company's offices, more modest and staid than those of the Preston Banking Company, yet equally tall and effective. On the other side more chemists, hairdressers, upholsterers, drapers, and glovers' shops; and here Butler's shop, full of Roman Catholic accessories, sculptured and pictorial crucifixes—ivory,

Opposite Arkwright House and Preston Minster. *David B. Prowse.*

The Harris Museum and Art Gallery dominates Preston's Market Square. *David B. Prowse.*

The façade and cupola are all that remain of the old Public Hall in Lune Street.
David B. Prowse.

David B. Prowse

ebony, brown wood, and bronze crucifixes of all imaginable sizes—by the side of the Kendal Bank. By the side of the Lancaster Bank is a very narrow street of very low houses, occupied by surveyors, land agents, valuers, a beadle, a sheriff's officer, a beer-shop, and a tailor; down which flakes of soot are flying and settling on the cracked, bad pavement, in which channels are made in communication with external wooden spouting to the houses. Beyond this, among the smart shops in Fishergate, stands a thatched house, with bulged plaster walls—the last vestige of old Preston in this bustling stream of modern traffic. Past the Shelley's Arms there is a very neat butcher's shop, formed of three round arches with iron grilles and plate glass sliding windows. Within, the table top is covered with marble. If the walls were lined with white tiles, instead of coloured a dirty sallow brown, this would be a model of a butcher's shop, and prove that shop-fronts for this business can be made architecturally tasteful and suitable. More shops—feather-shops, baby linen warehouses, watchmakers; more courts—dismal, dirty Platt's Court; light and well-paved Woodcock's Court, scented with an aromatic malt-ous odour. The offices of the Preston Herald Company (limited) ; the offices of the Preston Chronicle opposite; Thorp, Bayless, & Thorp's great drapery establishment, with a row of ventilating funnels behind the iron balustrade over the shop-front; a narrow alley with "James Leigh, brewer," at one corner of it, and a small butcher's shop at the other, and a full ash-pit seen in the midst thereof from the main road. Then Cannon - street, branching off, with Hogg's fruit and game shop at the corner, where pheasants and hares hang in festoons; partridges, pine apples, grouse, and grapes are grouped very artistically; then mat and matting shops, china shops, and the Preston Guardian office, at the corner of new Cock's yard—which yard leads to the new Cock Inn, and is used as one wide urinal, the miserable pebble pavement being full of hollows of slops. At last the Townhall narrows the road, just where Cheapside leaves Fishergate at a right angle, and the market-place opens out in view. The Townhall is neither modern nor ancient; but is a dingy worn-out mansion. The entrance immediately faces an alley 3 or 4 feet wide, by the side of the "Legs of Man" inn, down which is a dirty perspective. Brewster and Burrowe's double shop is a noticeable feature from this point: it is a draper's shop below; and above, the first floor has been taken out and another shop front, displaying cabinetmaker's goods, placed in its stead. We are familiar with show-rooms over shops; but this is shop above shop. The rear of the Townhall is open to the market-place, and is ragged, tasteless, smoky, and dirty. Shop shutters are leaning against the ruined walls,

Opposite The impressive spire of St Walburgh's Church is the haunt of the rare peregrine falcon. *David B. Prowse.*

Cheapside Market Square. In the foreground is the obelisk which has now been reinstated. *The watercolours of Edwin Beattie (1845–1917) are reproduced with the kind permission of the Jesuit Community at St Wilfrid's, Preston.*

as are temporary wooden urinals; and placards and posters are stuck upon every available space.

The market-place is a handsome roomy parallelogram, surrounded on two sides by good shops, inns, and hotel; by the Townhall on the third; and by a row of shops on the fourth side, which is broken up by alleys leading to the shambles in the rear of them. Hay seeds, hay, and straw, are scattered over the pebble pavements; and on the off market-days the great open space is occupied by a few odd vegetable stalls on trestles, with movable wooden canopies. As we look on, a rag fair is held—one man selling remnants of highly-coloured, painted and glazed calico, odd bits of cloth, fragments of white linen; another man selling every possible description of cheap haberdashery, reels of cotton, combs, pins, needles, &c.; and both spread their wares upon the ground. It is impossible to be unimpressed with the capabilities of the site. If the Townhall were rebuilt; the row of shops with the butchers' shambles in their rear, with all the narrow courts intersecting this block of building, removed, and a meat market built instead; the block of houses on the north side of the market-place removed, and a general market built on its site; Preston would be able to boast of one of the finest market-places in the kingdom. We were glad to hear that the market committee were in consultation with Mr. G. G. Scott upon this

16

subject. But the drainage and paving should not be overlooked in favour of more showy accommodation. The gutters in the market-place run with slops thrown out of the houses in the courts around; channels across the pavement in Clayton-court—channels from urinals in a passage to the Blue Anchor—channels in passage to Strait Shambles,—all furnish tributaries to the stream down the market kennel. Wilcockson's-court does the same: Ginbow entry, leading to the Wheat-sheaf and White Hart, brings down the swimmings from exposed urinals and stable muck; and washings from the shambles are flowing down all the livelong day. Strait shambles, one of the passage ways in the block of shambles, may be taken as a type of the rest,—lines of close butchers' shops, running at right angles from the market, with a dark living-room in the rear of each, and a smaller and darker sleeping-room above. The washings from the blocks are finding channels down to the lowest level; losing on the way great part of their bulk, which is absorbed into the soil. And so we pick our way round to the principal facade of the shambles in Lancaster-row. This is recessed back: the upper part projects over the lower, and is supported on rude, monolithic, tapering pillars, out of the perpendicular. The brickwork above is dirty white where it is not dirty black: the windows are very small, and filled with small panes; and the whole place has an uncouth and unclean appearance.

The old Shambles and the Shoulder of Mutton Inn. Alongside is Gin Bow Entry.
The watercolours of Edwin Beattie (1845–1917) are reproduced with the kind permission of the Jesuit Community at St Wilfrid's, Preston.

The post-office is near the shambles, and contrasts very favourably with them, being in a block of newly-erected lofty houses exactly opposite : it is roomy and convenient. Attached to the Stanley Arms, in the same block, is a notice-board, inscribed, "Police regulations. Make no wet." And yet at the end of the hotel there is an unprotected urinal; and, unprovided for by drainage, the urine flows across the pavement in a broad stream.

A long, old-fashioned, winding thoroughfare, called Friargate, straggles away down hill from the market-place. This is a long tortuous street, of second and third rate shops, to supply the wants of the dwellers in the innumerable courts and alleys with which it is intersected. In the main street scavenage does not appear to be thought of; and in the alleys and courts the laws of boards of health are set at defiance. The rear premises of both sides of Friargate, which is about a mile long, and, starting from the market-place, is in the centre of the town, are horrible masses of corruption and forcing pits for fever. In Fishwick's-yard there are three vile privies and a crammed offal-pit close to the wretched houses, which, with their broken paved and damp floors are scarcely fit for human habitation: and the overflowings from slops of another row of houses run down the yard. 'Four more dreadful pits at the end near a back lane are piled full, and leak across the alley into Friargate. These are the characteristics of all the courts and passages in the neighbourhood: some of them, such as Hardman's-yard, at the corner of the newly-painted Waterloo Inn, are whitened and made showy to look clean about the entrances ; but step past the whitewash near the street, and you will find, as in this case, a monster midden pit, with privies at each end, open to the front of a whole row of houses whose inhabitants they serve. The clothes of the poor people are actually hanging to dry over this disgusting pit; and the pebble pavement around is befouled by the children in the yard, for whom no provision whatever has been made. Peelings, slops, tea-leaves, are strewn about the yard. This pit, of awful dimensions, receives the whole of the refuse from the various families in the row; which lies there rotting for weeks and months, and is then disturbed and carried through into the main street. We noted at the lowest point next Friargate a shutter up to indicate a death. In Milling's-yard [Melling's-yard], a little farther off, matters were a little better, as there were gratings at intervals through which liquid refuse passed away; but at each of these there were collections of solid filth around, which could not get through, and yet were not swept away. The semi-circular apse end of St. George's Church, full of richly-painted glass, is within a dozen feet of the poor homes in this yard: clothes-lines are tied to the church-yard railings, and a quantity of clothes hangs fluttering, like

18

The old Preston Town Hall built in 1782 looking towards Church Street.
The watercolours of Edwin Beattie (1845–1917) are reproduced with the kind permission of the Jesuit Community at St Wilfrid's, Preston.

banners, over the graves. The church-yard is, properly, closed. The church is but a travestie of Norman work,—the tower-porch, something between a porch and a tower, being in marvellously bad taste. There are plenty more yards on both sides of the road,—Tayler's-yard, Brown's-yard, Cradwell's-yard [Gradwell's-yard], with "lodgings for travellers:" and all the kennels are running with slops and mud. A space bounded by Chapel-yard is so cribbed and confined, that the rear premises of respectable shops and privies and ash-pits jostle each other in the smallest space that could by any stretch of imagination be called a yard; and over these the inhabitants have to hang their linen to dry. A passage before coming to Union-street has a marine store and rag and bone shop at one end and a candlemaker's at the other; and in Union-street flows a kennel full of moist filth, slops, and tea-leaves, which has a slow current into Friarsgate.

In the rear of Snow-hill there is another similar neighbourhood: oyster-shells are strewn about, and the ground is the common privy for children. Pawnbrokers and marine-store dealers flourish around.

High-street is a row of poor houses, about one-eighth of a mile long, with small back yards; and at the back of these a huge sewer positively discharges itself on to the surface, and forms a wide bog, the whole length of the row of houses. The solid filth from this overflows the outlets, and stops up the privies of the High-street residents; and to see an old woman raking in the filth to find the sewer was a pitiable spectacle. A man, standing by, remarked that it had been nearly as bad as that for nine years, to his knowledge— " never anything but a bog, even in summer,"— but that, since Peader & Lever had begun to boil tripe at the top of the street, and throw their boiling greasy water on to the sewage, it was daily getting worse. It must be observed that this is not a made ditch. The Board of Health— or, more correctly speaking, of Illness — has brought a sewer up to the high end of the street, and then discharged its contents, to make its own way. As the ground falls the sewage has made a course for itself; and the overflowings from aged pigsties,middens, and pits, belonging to the houses in High-street, have run into it in tributary streams! The back windows of the houses overlook a large plot of ground in a transitory condition, known by tradition only, as the Orchard, which is partly built upon and partly used as a play-ground by the "roughs." A spacious Methodist free church and free schools are planted in the midst; while, in another part of it, a permanent wooden circus has been set up, which looks like a vast conical tumulus, or an aboriginal's hut. The rest of the Orchard is a surface of thick, black, hard mud, on which men are playing at "putting the stone" and "pitch and toss," and on which a tribe of pigs are disporting pork fashion. Great holes are worn in this muddy play-ground, and pools of offensive colour and odour finish the landscape.

Preston Guild Walk

Start/finish   Market Square, Preston town centre
Distance   I mile (1.6 kilometres)
Time   2 hours
Grade   Easy
General   Park & Ride facilities available at Strand Road and
                Walton-le-Dale

The Preston Guild walk begins in the Market Square and then proceeds through the elaborate Miller Arcade to Fishergate at its junction with Church Street. Turn left to the minster and right along Stoneygate to Arkwright House.

For centuries Preston Guild has been associated with civic, commercial and cultural events in the town. During more genteel times the affluent were able to afford sedan chairs, first introduced during the guild of 1622. Thereafter they rode in them to church on Sundays and were carried to balls and private parties, whilst sedately travelling hither and thither around the town carrying out their business. The last passenger ride in a sedan chair was made c. 1850, twelve years after the first railway arrived in Preston.

We begin with a short walk through part of the city centre, with a focus on buildings which have an association with past guild events. The walk integrates parts of the first three main thoroughfares of Preston: Church (Gate) Street, with its imposing minster; Fishergate, so named because it led to a ford of the river Ribble at Penwortham Holme and its medieval salmon fisheries; and Friargate, a route from the market place to Preston Moor and on to the Fylde, and aptly alluding to the site of a thirteenth-century Franciscan Abbey that was situated near Marsh Lane. In medieval times burgages of land suitable for a dwelling were granted to the burgesses on admission to the Guild Merchant – thus we have a link with one of the earliest of the Preston guilds. Churchgate, Fishergate and Friargate are three of the earliest examples of this connection, evidenced by a pattern of narrow strips of land extending rearwards and further exemplified by the site of the former Royal Hippodrome Theatre on Friargate, now Wilkinsons. This department store occupies a defined plot forming a whole ancient pattern of land, other vestiges of which may also be traced by a discerning eye on both Church Street and Fishergate.

We commence at Preston's ancient Market Square, which is dominated by great public buildings including the Cenotaph, the Sessions House, Harris Museum and Art Gallery, Miller Arcade and the old Post Office, though sadly there is one serious omission. The Gothic Town Hall designed by George Gilbert Scott and built in 1867 was seriously damaged by fire in March 1947 and though part of the building was used for a time it was subsequently completely demolished in 1962. Significantly, the foundation stone of the Town Hall had been laid with appropriate pomp and ceremony during the Preston Guild week of September 1862. The loss of the distinctive landmark tower prominent on the skyline of Preston, and the original Guild Hall with its capacity for 1,000 patrons as a venue for public meetings, balls, concert recitals and historic Guild Courts, was a heartbreaking wrench for many Prestonians.

Preston architect James Hibbert designed the Grade I listed Harris Museum and Art Gallery, founded by local solicitor Edmund Richard Harris whose legacy of £30,000 was left for charitable and cultural purposes for the people of Preston. This superb unmodified building is in my opinion the finest in Lancashire and stands aloft, resembling a Greek temple with its six Greek Ionic columns supporting a pediment with classical figures. Beneath them a dedication, suggesting the promotion of mental awareness and knowledge with the words 'to literature, arts and science' – though not apparently history! Hibbert travelled extensively in Europe to gain inspiration for the building, which is said to resemble the original Berlin Opera House. It is perhaps ironic that the chosen site for the new building led to 'The Shambles' – an historic network of narrow passages and a medley of quaint seventeenth-century buildings including seven hostelries – being swept away. Nevertheless the foundation stone for the Harris was laid to coincide with the guild celebration of 1882 and although completed around six years later the great building was not officially opened until 1893. The building incorporates lending and reference libraries; an art gallery with English paintings from the eighteenth century such as the well-known portrait of 'Pauline in the Yellow Dress' by James Gunn; the Egyptian Balcony – high up on the top deck; a museum with a collection of English ceramics, costumes and items of outstanding local interest such as coins from the Cuerdale Hoard, a dugout canoe from the newly excavated Preston Dock and the renowned 'Poulton Elk', a much admired feature of the museum with prehistoric origins. The old bull elk is due for a change of habitat to a brand new gallery focusing on the history of Preston, the opening of which is fittingly scheduled to coincide with Preston Guild 2012.

Another structure associated with the guilds of yesteryear is the Obelisk, a colossal Gothic stone pillar which was erected on the Market Square to be ready for the guild of 1782. It was removed in 1853 and after many years languishing elsewhere was subsequently restored and re-established on the Market Square. It was then unveiled by Her Majesty Queen Elizabeth II on 10 May 1979, in celebration of the town's octocentenary. Close to the Obelisk is a rather more shameful link with the diverse history of the Market Square. It is a circular stone enclosing an iron ring that prior to 1835 was used in the grotesque sport of tethered bull baiting. The occupier of Preston's oldest trading outlet, the extant tiny half-timbered jeweller's shop situated on nearby Cheapside and originating over 360 years ago, would have had a grandstand view, had he wanted it!

To the south of the Market Square is Miller Arcade. This ornate building is adorned by an Italian terracotta-style façade and was built for a local dentist, Nathaniel Miller, in 1903. The centre of the shopping emporium was a traditional meeting point for courting couples, including yours truly!

The Market Square has long been at the forefront of political and commercial life. In the shadow of a succession of town halls Prestonians have welcomed monarchs, statesmen and famous personalities, celebrated momentous occasions, visited innumerable fairs and attended a diverse range of Preston Guild events. Entering Church Street from Miller Arcade we may take the opportunity to visit the historic minster that was dedicated to St John the Divine in the sixteenth century. The minster was completely rebuilt between 1853 and 1855 with a steeple embellishing the original tower. Significantly the permanence of a parish church on this conspicuous site dates back to before the Norman Invasion. We know that an earlier Saxon church was dedicated to St Wilfrid which implies that the church is probably as old as Preston (the name deriving from 'priest town') itself. Saint Wilfrid's crest, the sacraficial lamb and the letters 'PP', standing for Prince of Peace, was adopted as the town's coat of arms. Another significant milestone in the history of the parish church followed the grant of city status to Preston in 2002. Thereafter the church was reordered and the following year became the minster.

Sir Richard Arkwright revolutionised the textile industry, so after admiring the parish church why not take a short walk down Stoneygate past the 'Old Cockpit', associated with Joseph Livesey and the Temperance cause, to Arkwright House, to see for yourself the birthplace of the Industrial Revolution, now happily restored and currently occupied by Age Concern.

Retrace your steps and commence walking down Fishergate past Guildhall Street (left). Wander along Fishergate towards the railway station and then retrace your steps, turning left into Lune Street.

Guildhall Steet was so named because of its proximity to the Guild Hall (within the old Town Hall) and the impending guild of 1882. Meanwhile Boots the Chemist on the corner of Guildhall Street occupies the site of New Cock Yard and a pub bearing the same name which first opened its doors to customers in 1795.

As an ornithological aside, the scarce little black redstart has been spotted intermittently over the last few years in the vicinity of Guildhall Street, tending to haunt the exterior of high buildings between here and the minster. The ubiquitious pied wagtail can also be seen around here. These dapper black and white birds do what their name implies as they scurry around streets, open areas and car parks during the daylight hours. At dusk they may be seen flying to the city's trees and buildings to roost communally. Also sharing the urban environment in Preston are flocks of starling and a few house sparrows, although such is the course of 'progress' that both of these formerly common birds have become of conservation concern, and are now officially listed as red data species. The city centre has regular flocks of feral pigeon which provide a source of prey for the the rare peregrine falcon, now domiciled on

The magnificent Harris Museum and Art Gallery shortly after construction in the late Victorian era. To the left is the Municipal Building. *Courtesy of Longridge & District Local History Society.*

the impressive high spire of St Walburgh's to the north. Waxwings have made a guest appearance in front of the façade of the Corn Exchange, as when the berry crop fails in Scandinavia flocks of them invade Britain in search of food. During a good waxwing winter these charismatic birds form roving flocks and are to be found feeding especially on the berries of rowan and cotoneaster wherever there are plentiful supplies, in and around the city.

Moving on we pass the entrance to St George's Shopping Centre that was developed in 1976 to replace a much earlier version of a shopping centre that embraced Bamber's Yard and Anchor Court, situated between Fishergate and Friargate. Just beyond Lune Street, Preston's illustrious Theatre Royal once stood on Fishergate at the junction of the appropriately named Theatre Street and was associated with many guilds. Indeed its opening coincided with Preston Guild 1802 at a time when Preston was still dominated by lawyers, doctors, merchants, shopkeepers and bankers and increasingly, wealthy mill owners. During over 180 years of entertainment it played host to countless legendary names of stage and screen. The Preston historian, Whittle, alluded to Preston Guild and the Theatre Royal in 1821: 'It is hoped that this place will be resorted to during the ensuing guild year, 1822, by those ladies and gentlemen visiting the town during this grand fête; no doubt able performers will be brought down from the metropolis, for the purpose of giving éclat to this festival, celebrated every twentieth year.' Preston architect James Hibbert extensively re-designed the Theatre Royal in 1869 and gave it a Regency-style façade, which was improved and further embellished to celebrate the 1882 Preston Guild. A grand re-opening night, followed by different performances each night of the guild, consisted of military bands and three companies presenting opera and dramatic performances. Remarkably, Franz Lizst, Niccolò Paganini, Oscar Wilde and Sir Henry Irving also delighted audiences there during the nineteenth century.

Across the road from the theatre James Hibbert also designed the Baptist Chapel, with its prominent clock tower, which was completed in 1858 and has always been a familiar landmark on Fishergate. Meanwhile on Lune Street, during December 1821, building work commenced on the Corn Exchange, and on 22 September 1822, the partially completed building celebrated its first guild in an adjacent temporary structure. It was not until June 1824 that the Corn Exchange was officially opened by the Mayor of Preston. The façade of the original Corn Exchange remains to this day as the entrance to a public house bearing the same name and incorporating the original iron gates that once opened onto the butter market. In the centre stood a large grain and vegetable market that was later transformed into the Public Hall auditorium, now sadly demolished. During guild year 1882 the original Corn exchange was extended and rebuilt as the Public Hall, a venue for public meetings, exhibitions and musical entertainment. With capacity for 3,500 it was one of the largest public halls in Lancashire. Captain J. Norwood presented his annual concerts with vocalists and maintained the orchestral tradition for over forty years.

Preston guilds have long been associated with lavish productions. This is exemplified by a concert series of famous international performers launched at the old Public Hall to celebrate Preston Guild 1922:

'International Celebrity Subscription Concerts'
Preston Guild, 1 September 1922

The Directors have the honour to announce
their 1922–1923 record series.

Last appearance of Tetrazzini –
world famous Queen of song for a long period

Clara Butt and Kennerley Rumford, direct from the triumphs of their world tour
Kreisler – the world's master violinist

Last appearance prior to world tour: Pachman –
Whose art stands alone

Pouishnoff – the world famous Polish pianist:
Stella Power – the little Melba

Aileen D'Orme –
re-appearance of this brilliant vocalist on the concert platform

Lamara –
the celebrated Californian nightingale

Eric Marshall –
the celebrated English baritone

Melsa –
direct from a tour of three continents

During the twentieth century many leading artists and politicians performed here and the Public Hall heralded several guilds with the ritual of the historic Guild Court. In 1962 an obscure pop group from Liverpool was paid £18 to appear at the Public Hall on the occasion of the annual Preston Grasshoppers Rugby Club Dance. They even returned to the hall the following year for another gig but this time to wide acclaim. They were called 'The Beatles', and the rest, as they say, is history!

From Lune Street turn right into Friargate and back to the starting point of the walk in the Market Square.

Walking up Friargate the awe-inspiring sight of the Harris Museum and Art Gallery gradually unfolds as a Victorian masterpiece dominating the Market Square. On the left is the Black Horse pub, the present building dating back to 1898 and still retaining its Victorian charm and artefacts. In fact, the bar, comprising beautiful ceramics and Art Nouveau stained glass, is outstanding and Grade II listed by English Heritage – the beer is good too! It is on record that alcoholic beverages sustained a plethora of artists appearing next door at the Royal Hippodrome from 1905 until the final curtain fell at the old music hall in 1957. The years between 1905 and 1914 were the town's golden years of variety, with many great music hall performers appearing on stage. Returning to the Market Square Giles Gilbert Scott probably gained inspiration from the Whitehall Cenotapth to design Preston's superb memorial to the fallen of The Great War. The Preston Cenotapth has taken pride of place in the Market Square since it was installed in 1926 and unveiled by Lord Jellicoe. During the present guild year it has been announced that it is justifiably to undergo extensive restoration and given more prominence.

Walking alongside the Municipal Building next to Harris Street we catch a glimpse of Preston Guild Hall, comprising a concert venue and a theatre.

Preston parish church of St John before the steeple was added *c.* 1853.
The watercolours of Edwin Beattie (1845–1917) are reproduced with the kind permission of the Jesuit Community at St Wilfrid's, Preston.

The city's popular entertainment industry has developed from humble beginnings. During the 1842 guild, for example, Pablo Fondue's travelling Circus Royal came to Preston. The admission prices during guild week were doubled for a superior company of male and female equestrians, the diminutive fairy ponies (Albert and Nelson), and ropedancers. Management claimed the 'first female equestrians in the world'. Following the guild the circus re-opened and members of the public were given the opportunity to see the circus at the old prices – front boxes, 2s., side boxes 1s., pit 6d., and gallery 3d. These prices would still have been unaffordable for many in 1842.

Music hall has its origins in events such as this and by the time of the 1882 guild and the opening of the rebuilt Preston Railway Station two years earlier the original Gaiety Temperance Theatre had stood in the way of the proposed railway station expansion into Butler Street and was demolished. Sole proprietor, Henry Hemfrey, transferred to new premises, situated in Tithebarn Street, complete with fixed pit and gallery seats and a properly equipped stage with capacity for 2,000 patrons. Thus was born Preston's first commodious purpose-built music hall for staging predominantly generic variety and circus entertainment. Significantly the opening of the new Gaiety Palace Theatre of Varieties coincided with the September guild of 1882 and included midnight performances of the grand Guild Company. Preston's magnificent Park Hotel overlooking Avenham Park was also completed in time for guild week 1882 and a large painting of the hotel featured on the curtain drop during the opening night of the music hall.

The opening of the Gaiety in 1882 marked a significant point in national music hall development. Preston's mid-ninteenth-century pub singing saloons decamped to three major variety theatres, built between 1905 and 1913, towards the end of the national music hall boom. By the beginning of the twentieth century the coming of the cinema posed a significant threat to the music hall scene, paradoxically a subject which featured in the programme when the Gaiety Theatre changed its identity to become the Princes Theatre during the Edwardian era.

We are again reminded of Preston Guild with the advent of silent movies during the twentieth century and the pertinently named 'Guild Cinema', on Geoffrey Street, which was opened for the 1922 guild and remained a cinema until 1959. The Guild Hall complex was planned to be ready for the 1972 guild, but, owing to industrial action by the builders, the new building was not completed in time and all events were quickly transferred to the Public Hall. Many famous performers from the world of show business, popular and classical music have featured in concert performances at the Guild Hall and its predecessor, the Public Hall of 1882. My recollections of

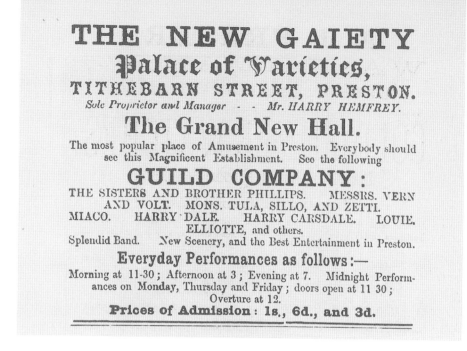

The New Gaiety Palace of Varieties celebrated Preston Guild 1882 at the time of its opening with propaganda and a generic music hall programme. *Author's collection.*

guild events include a concert by Vera Lynn and all the pomp and ceremony of the Guild Court which took place in the large auditorium. Throughout the 1972 guild the Public Hall played a major part in the guild festivities and it seemed ironic that the Public Hall should end as it began in 1822, playing host to a guild, albeit a swan song for the old trooper! The new Guild Hall was subsequently opened on 9 November 1972 and the first public performance was that of the 'Little Angels of Korea'.

Moving on to the present day and coinciding with the 2012 guild, is the establishment of the 'Preston Guild Wheel' and the new Brockholes Nature Reserve. The Guild Wheel is a new twenty-one mile cycleway/walkway around Preston, mostly off road, which links the city to the countryside and will turn out to be a fine legacy of Preston Guild 2012. It will undoubtedly promote health and recreation and will be popular with cyclists, walkers and runners and be easily accessible to wheelchair users. To add diversity and encourage more use of the Wheel, impressive monuments depicting great events in local and national history will be built along the route, which provide an attractive linear park with a wildlife, plant and tree corridor. It will also pass close by the Brockholes Reserve, a newly created habitat there to be enjoyed by families as well as discerning birdwatchers and naturalists which is owned and managed by the Lancashire Wildlife Trust. Grab your binoculars! This is a top birdwatching and wildlife site and is fully described on page 47.

Trains & Boats & Birds

Start/finish	Start and finish at the public car park near Morrisons
Grid Ref	513295
Distance	4 miles (6.4 kilometres)
Time	2–3 hours
Grade	Easy
General	Refreshment, toilet and parking facilities at the marina

We now move out of the town centre and explore another part of Preston's natural history and heritage. This walk takes in the Preston Marina and a tidal section of the river Ribble, where good birdwatching may be enjoyed to the Millennium Link – the farthest point of the walk. At times the footpath runs parallel to the splendid Ribble Steam Railway, allowing good views of this popular operational railway, hence the walk's title, trains and boats and birds.

From Morrisons proceed to the modern swing bridge at the dock entrance – not surprisingly a renowned haunt of steam-railway photographers – to take the signed Riverside Walk/Guild Wheel. From here walk west following the Guild Wheel signs along the north bank of the river via the curiously named 'Bull Nose' and the steam-railway centre. Just before a junction with the Guild Wheel and Wallend Road, branch left through an iron gate. Thereafter the path gradually becomes less obvious but perseverance will lead you past a go-kart/motor-cycle circuit and onto the confluence of Savick Brook, nowadays known as the Millennium Link. A raised embankment gives an uninterrupted view of the channel and marshes. At the confluence it is recommended you walk inland to view the adjacent Ashton Marsh before retracing your steps to the marina with further opportunities to view the Ribble, ideally at a different state of the tide. There is a track (of sorts) that leads along the north side of the go-kart circuit and provides an alternative circular route back.

Opposite Flocks of black-tailed godwit haunt the estuarine mud flats and Ribble marshes during winter and early spring. *Courtesy of Peter Smith.*

An immature Iceland gull stands forlorn on a frozen Preston Dock. *Courtesy of Peter Smith.*

New industries were founded when W. Dick and J. Kerr established their engineering works in 1897 to meet the growing demand for new tramcars and railway locomotives. This became one of the town's major twentieth-century employers with a workforce of over 10 per cent of the male workers of the town, as against 23 per cent in all branches of cotton. In October 1846, a railway branch line was constructed from the North Union Preston Station to serve the Victoria Quay on the river Ribble, via a steep gradient of 1 in 29. The line was extended to serve the new Preston Docks in 1882 and gratifyingly it continues to be used for commercial freight and is operated for public enjoyment by the Ribble Steam Railway's dedicated team of enthusiasts. The steam railway is well worth a visit by the way, and ideal for families and children, who love the Thomas the Tank Engine friendly engine weekends. Details of all scheduled events including steam and diesel gala weekends can be obtained on the website: www.ribblesteamrail.org.uk.

Long before the Albert Edward Dock was opened in 1892 a new riverside quay was opened in 1825 to cater for an increase in shipping. In 1828 the first of a new generation of steamships, the *St David*, navigated the river. The Victoria Quay was opened for commercial trading as early as 1839 and three years later the Port of Preston was officially recognised. The *Preston Guardian* of 1845 provides an illuminating insight into what was then a busy port with plenty of activity and lots of tall sailing ships: 'The New Quay was so thronged that the schooners were obliged to lie three deep ... We observed 22 vessels at their stations.' Preston also had its own shipbuilding industry with several riverside yards manufacturing a range of wooden, iron and even concrete vessels as well as a ship-breaking yard. Towards the end of the nineteenth century the landscape of Preston was transformed by the mammoth engineering task of diverting the course of the river Ribble to the south of the newly constructed dock basin. A major archaeological find was made deep beneath the surface of the riverbed yielding evidence of prehistoric wildlife and artefacts. A 'head count' comprised of thirty human skulls, over a hundred skulls of red deer, several wild ox, two pilot whale skulls, a bronze spearhead and two dug-out canoes. The collection has found a home in the Harris Museum at Preston and research findings indicate that this material has probably accumulated since the Bronze Age.

Preston Dock was opened for commercial trading during 1892, consolidating Preston's key position in the transport sector. The Albert Edward Dock was the largest single dock basin in the world when built, albeit at a distance of 16 miles from the Ribble estuary at Lytham St Annes, an obstacle which led to its ultimate closure. Throughout its existence the dock harboured only cargo vessels, with the exception of a few organised ferry trips on the distinctive ships of the Isle of Man Steam Packet Company, which came and went on the high tide. Shipping along the course of the Ribble was entirely tide dependent and the channel had to be dredged regularly at high tide by a fleet of ancient steam dredgers that were mainly named after the river Ribble and its tributaries. The unceasing silting of the channel and estuary combined with poor trade figures led to unsustainable financial losses and the Preston Corporation made the decision to close

A Bagnall 0-6-0 steam locomotive on Preston Dock *c*. 1968. *Courtesy of Stan Withers.*

the dock in October 1976, with the loss of 350 jobs, and to implement the Preston Dock Closure Act, 1981. During that year the legislation was enacted only nine days after the departure of the last commercial vessel to use the dock, which melancholic honour was somewhat poignantly given to a sand dredger.

Witnessing the activity of a busy commercial port with its assortment of vessels moored around the basin certainly made a very interesting day out. I well remember the dock in the 1950s and '60s when there was a flourishing trade in coal and timber and the regular interesting vessels such as the quaint tramp steamer *Helen Craig*, the little steam tugboat *Lucas*, gleaming white banana boats from the Caribbean bearing the names, *Leeward Islands* and *Windward Islands*. Then there were the very first roll-on/roll-off car ferries, *Empire Nordic*, *Empire Doric*, *Empire Cedric* and others in the same fleet that were later superseded by the *Bardic Ferry* and *Ionic Ferry* that regularly plied between Preston and Larne, Northern Ireland.

A favourite ship of mine was the humble little steam ship SS *Helen Craig* which was built in Belfast in 1891 and worked between Preston and Belfast thrice weekly for an incredible fifty years. Throughout her undistinguished career she carried a cargo of stinking animal bones from abattoirs at Belfast to Preston. Not surprisingly, *Helen* was infamous to generations of dockers, who knew her quite well for her distinctive shape and features, not to mention fragrances. She was affectionately known by them as 'th'owd bo'oan boat', which less glamorously translates as 'the old bone boat'. The tiny vessel was invariably heralded by swarming flocks of scavenging gull that were attracted to the maggots and other delightful gourmet delicacies that comprised the dubious cargo. Her inglorious routine was interrupted by dramatic events in December 1936, when she ran aground in the Ribble estuary at Peet's Light during a westerly gale. The Lytham lifeboat struggled to get alongside but managed to save all 11 crew members. Following a series of complex attempts to rescue the stricken ship she was re-floated and towed to Preston by one of the steam dredgers. Undaunted she survived another 25 years, but finally on 19 November 1959 her master circumnavigated the Ribble channel for the last time with a one-way ticket home to Belfast and finally Cork for an ignominious scrapping.

Many Prestonians will remember the former Isle of Man ferry, TSS *Manxman*. This grand old vessel circumnavigated the river when it entered the dock in 1981 to become a floating nightclub. Sadly, in 1991 the owners decided to relocate the vessel and she was towed to Liverpool. Nowadays the Ribble is the domain of pleasure craft, although exceptionally, during 2010/11, a huge shallow-draught coaster the MV *River Carrier*, was used to

34

The *Bardic Ferry* sailing up river past Freckleton towards Preston Dock. *Author's collection.*

convey several giant transformers which were towed from Ellesmere Port to a riverside quay at Penwortham. This will probably turn out to be the last large commercial vessel to visit Preston.

Preston Dock was given a new lease of life after closure when it was transformed into the Riversway Docklands and Marina. The marina itself provides moorings and dedicated facilities for large ocean-going yachts and canal barges. The latter can now navigate the nearby Millennium Link which successfully links with the nation's canal network. Alongside this development supermarkets, shops, restaurants and waterside walks have grown up. There is a signed public footpath, Riverside Walk, which allows good views across the river and provides opportunities for birdwatching, though the dock basin itself is always worth a look. The tidal river with associated salt marsh and exposed mud, is exploited by gulls, terns, waders and wildfowl. Numbers vary throughout the year and with the height and movements of the tide.

In winter cormorants and the occasional shag visit the basin and the former may also be seen flying along the channel, perching on the markers of the Ribble Navigation or standing on the mud with their wings hanging out to dry. Great crested grebes may be observed from time to time, both in the dock basin and on the river. On approaching the quay check the wintering gull flocks. The regular black-headed gull flocks may also contain Mediterranean gulls. Most of the gulls will take bread which allows a closer inspection. Scrutinise the larger gulls perched on the pontoons; most will be lesser

The veteran SS *Helen Craig* entering Preston Dock. *Courtesy of Stephen Sartin.*

black-backed, greater black-backed, herring and common gull but check for anything different including rarer species that occasionally visit the dock. A single ring-billed gull, a scarce visitor from North America, for example, made the Transatlantic crossing and successfully docked at Preston a few years ago, and during the winter of 2010/11 a first winter immature Iceland gull from the Arctic also found the basin to be a safe haven. This special winter visitor was content to forage for food on or just below the surface of the water and was also supplied with copious amounts of bread by visiting birdwatchers from near and afar. Despite the name, Iceland gulls breed in Iceland *and* Canada, and although rare in Lancashire, especially Preston, are relatively common winter visitors to the north-west coast of Scotland.

The man-made rafts have been positioned in the dock to provide a secure nesting site for common terns which may be seen flying over the basin and river channel from April into the summer. Along the Riverside Walk section of the route do not forget to check any trees, bushes and rough ground for any unsuspecting rarity that might just be lurking. Also check the old tide lines for wintering linnets and rock pipits, and at passage periods for meadow pipit, pied and white wagtails. During March look out for a ground-hopping little migrant with bags of character and a conspicuous white rump – the wheatear en route from Africa to upland breeding sites. The name is misleading as 'wheat' is actually an aberration of 'white', a reference to the bird's rump which is diagnostic and prominent in flight.

Many Prestonians will remember the TSS *Manxman*, seen here entering Preston Dock in 1981.
Courtesy of Peter Fitton.

As you progress along the riverside footpath, dense low stands of bramble are ideal for whitethroats. Listen out for their scolding sounds and song especially during late April. Linnets are still fairly common and the resident kestrel may be seen hovering over rough ground looking for small mammals. The remains of a large wooden pier are often frequented by cormorants strategically perched whilst assessing the fishing potential or resting between feeding. At low tide with mud and sand exposed there is usually a good selection of waders visible including oystercatcher, dunlin, curlew, redshank and in autumn small numbers of less common passage migrants such as greenshank, spotted redshank and even rarer species. During spring and autumn common sandpipers draw attention by their distinctive call and flight as they fly low over the surface of the water and perch with a bobbing and distinctive posture. When the tide starts to flow attention then shifts to the channel, where there are usually numbers of Canada geese, mallard, shelduck, teal, wigeon, goosander, a few goldeneye and great crested grebe.

A good vantage point is at the confluence of the Millennium Link and the adjacent Ashton Marsh, where the habitat of rough ground and willow scrub predictably harbours returning willow warblers from late April as well as numerous rabbits. The river, canal and coastal creeks are possible haunts of the kingfisher, which are sometimes seen outside the breeding season using posts as fishing perches. Black-tailed godwits haunt the edge of the river, marshes and adjacent fields. Grey herons are commonly seen

on the river and the Millennium Link, and within two kilometres of the confluence they build huge nests and raise their bizarre-looking youngsters at a tree-top heronry. As the tide comes in over the rapidly disappearing saltings, oystercatchers, curlews and redshanks feed continuously and flocks of shelduck, mallard, teal and lapwing are driven onto the Ribble marshes. Be careful with curlew identification during April and May; its smaller relative, the whimbrel, occurs on passage here in spring. At high tide calm descends on the assembled roosting flocks but any sense of a state of normality may be quickly shattered by the sudden appearance of a merlin or a local peregrine which nest on the spire of St Walburge's Church, Preston. Peregrines provoke instant panic in the massed ranks of smaller waders, creating a magnificent spectacle as the flocks weave and turn at great speed as the falcon attempts to outfly or stoop on its intended prey.

Opposite top   The TSS *Manxman* being towed away in 1991. *Courtesy of Peter Fitton.*

Opposite bottom   The *Hoveringham 4* was the last commercial vessel to depart from the Albert Edward Dock, Preston, before its closure in 1981. *Courtesy of Peter Fitton.*

Black-tailed godwit showing off its prominent white wing bar. *Courtesy of Peter Smith.*

Hoghton Tower, the River Darwen & the Leeds–Liverpool Canal

Start/finish	Start and finish at the Royal Oak, Riley Green, Hoghton
Grid Ref	621251
Distance	5 miles (8 kilometres)
Time	3–4 hours
Grade	Easy
General	Refreshment and toilet facilities at the Boatyard Inn and the Royal Oak at Riley Green
	Limited parking in Green Lane and the public house car park (for hotel patrons only). Hoghton Tower is one of the great stately homes of England and is open to the public during the summer months and on Bank Holiday weekends. For further details visit the website www.hoghtontower.co.uk or telephone 01254 852986

This walk commences in Green Lane adjacent to the Royal Oak at Riley Green situated on the A675 near Hoghton. Apart from birdwatching the walk has a great deal of interest, including the historic Hoghton Tower. The river Darwen is a particularly attractive feature of the walk, especially where it enters a spectacular gorge spanned by a railway viaduct. The walk also follows the towpath of the Leeds and Liverpool Canal between Feniscowles and the Boatyard Inn at Riley Green.

From the Royal Oak walk along Green Lane, following the waymarked footpath across fields, and cross over the drive leading to Hoghton Tower. Continue along the path adjacent to the perimeter wall of the Hoghton estate and pass

Opposite top The imposing front entrance to Hoghton Tower. *Courtesy of Phil Garlington.*

Opposite bottom A superb depiction of the viaduct straddling the river Darwen, complete with Victorian train. *Courtesy of Robert Gregson.*

through a wood, taking care as you cross over a pedestrian crossing of the main East Lancashire Railway line. Continue to follow the path that descends alongside a wood to a minor road. Turn left along the road and walk a short distance before taking a right at the junction with Valley Road. Walk to the end of Valley Road, to reach the hamlet of Hoghton Bottoms. Cross over a footbridge and immediately thereafter turn right along a footpath that parallels the river Darwen to a humpback bridge.

Cross over the bridge and turn left along the road to reach several cottages. Here the road becomes a footpath that takes you through the attractive Hoghton Gorge, resplendent with its weir. Pass beneath the colossal arched viaduct and continue to walk along the aptly named Witton Weavers' Way across fields to enter a wood. Emerging from the wood walk across fields and onto a track leading to the main Blackburn road, turn left along the A675 and walk a short distance downhill to the first public footpath sign on the right. The path takes you past the site of a former paper mill and eventually swings right up a bank onto the Leeds–Liverpool towpath. Turn right and walk along the towpath to bridge 91A, leave the towpath here and walk the short distance along the A674, Bolton road, back to the starting point of the walk at the Royal Oak.

Hoghton Tower, situated on a prominent and defensible hill-top position at the end of an imposing driveway and resembling a fairytale style castle, is one Lancashire's landmark attractions. It is the ancestral home of the de

Raven nest close to Hoghton Tower. *Courtesy of Peter Smith.*

Hoghton baronets and there are few of the landed aristocracy of England whose history goes as far back as that of this family. It is quite breathtaking to ascend the driveway and marvel at the gritstone building with its battlements and mullioned windows before entering the inner courtyard. Hoghton Tower's origins can be traced back to medieval times, c.1109, when the de Hoghton family held property in the township of Hoghton. By the time of the sixteenth century the de Hoghtons possessed extensive estates at Hoghton and elsewhere in the Ribble Valley. The Hoghton Tower of today was rebuilt by Sir Thomas Hoghton as a house, though resembling a castle, in 1565 on the site of an earlier fortification.

Significantly the notable building has played host to some very distinguished guests and is famously said to be the place where William Shakespeare spent his lost years at the start of his working life. Overall the evidence amongst leading academic historians supports the theory that he did reside there, and at other Lancashire noblemen's houses, during the Renaissance.

In 1617 Sir Richard Hoghton invited King James I to stay at Hoghton Tower for three days, along with a plethora of dukes, earls and knights, to indulge in a spot of hunting complete with a splendid banquet. During the course of the feast the king was said to be so impressed by a loin of beef that he knighted it 'Sir Loin', hence the name roast sirloin of beef. A copy of the dinner menu served to the king can be seen in the great hall which is dominated by the impressive minstrels' gallery. In summer the atmosphere is further enhanced by the Tudor gardens, grounds and courtyards. Hoghton Tower is the present seat of Sir Bernard de Hoghton.

Apart from its illustrious heritage the Hoghton estate is not without ornithological merit and two of its most interesting birds, the raven and peregrine falcon, may be seen or heard from the peripheral open areas surrounding the estate. Look up for ravens on hearing trumpet-like notes; this, the largest member of the crow family, often flies in tandem, engaging in a spectacular display. Sparrowhawk and kestrel may often be seen over fields and favoured habitats, hunting for small birds and mammals respectively.

The woodlands and gardens lining the river Darwen have buzzard, chaffinch, goldfinch, bullfinch, nuthatch, treecreeper, jay and wood pigeon. At Hoghton Bottoms check the birdfeeding stations for visiting common birds and perhaps an opportunistic great spotted woodpecker feeding on fat balls. During springtime listen out for the blackbird's song whilst walking alongside the river Darwen and next to gardens and woodland fringe. In spring willow warblers arrive shortly after the chiffchaff, whose distinctive 'chiff-chaff chiff-chaff' can be heard in the higher trees. These two species appear similar but the song is totally different. Blackcaps often sing from the higher trees but only a trained ear will distinguish their song from that of the garden warbler, which is generally longer, more melodic and less strident.

Upstream from Hoghton Bottoms the swift-flowing river passes through a picturesque woodland gorge, further enhanced by a weir and the grandeur of a three-arched railway viaduct rising from the riverbed to a height of 108 feet. The viaduct was completed in time for the opening of the Preston to Blackburn Railway on 1 June 1846 and is unquestionably an admirable feat of Victorian engineering. Down below in the vicinity of the waterfall is a good place to see the aquatic dipper, perhaps nesting and doing precisely what its name implies – bobbing about like clockwork and dipping into an increasingly less polluted river Darwen. Look out for kingfisher, sand martin, pied and grey wagtail, which are all fairly regular along the river. Fortunately hitherto polluted rivers like the Darwen have been cleaned up during the last twenty years, as a result of better regulation and investment by the Environment Agency and water industry, and calmer stretches upstream of the weir now hold moorhen, mallard and goosander. Leaving the Darwen behind the footpath branches off through woods to reach the main road on the outskirts of Feniscowles.

The walk along the canal towpath is attractive though alas not very 'birdy'. Kingfishers are seen occasionally flying over the placid waters of the Leeds–Liverpool Canal but you may have to make do with the resident motley collection of hybrid mallard and Canada geese. Good hunting!

Opposite   A delightful study of a goldfinch. *Courtesy of Peter Smith.*

Nowadays the river Darwen is the haunt of the endearing kingfisher. *Courtesy of Peter Smith.*

Brockholes Nature Reserve
Birdwatching & Heritage

The reserve is situated at Salmesbury near to the A59 on the north bank of the Ribble and just off Junction 31 of the M6. Follow the reserve signs from the A59 and cross an occupation bridge alongside the motorway. There is a large paying car park though there is no admission charge to the reserve or village centre where refreshments, toilet and other facilities are provided. The centre is open April to October until 17:00 hours and from November to March until 16:00 hours. It should be noted that dogs are not allowed on the reserve as they can disturb and harm wildlife. However, assistance dogs are allowed on the reserve if under close supervision. Allow four to eight hours to enjoy the facilities and walks.

There are three waymarked walks incorporating bird hides on the reserve and the Ribble Way public footpath and combined Guild Wheel cycleway – where dogs may be taken – bisects the reserve. There are facilities for the disabled with wheelchair access to walks. Guided walks of the reserve are available throughout the year.

This chapter describes the natural history and history of Brockholes Reserve and incorporates three suggested walks. The wooded areas along the river Ribble have been growing here for thousands of years and are designated as ancient woodlands. Boilton, Red Scar and Tun Brook (or Tunbrook) woods form part of the largest complex of semi-natural woodland in the Lancashire plains and valleys, though it was not until 1979, at the suggestion of the Lancashire Naturalists Trust, that the Nature Conservancy Council (now Natural England) first scheduled them as a Site of Special Scientific Interest.

At a time when the odd pair of yellow wagtail still attempted to nest on un-improved pasture, Brockholes Quarry began to be excavated

Opposite Marshy areas at Brockholes Reserve are home to the intriguing mouse-like grasshopper warbler. *Courtesy of Peter Smith.*

on the north bank of the river in close proximity to the M6 motorway. Although development of the site for gravel extraction was initially opposed by the Lancashire Wildlife Trust, the potential for a major new nature reserve was soon realised following the cessation of quarrying. The basic concept was that if someone wants to dig a hole in the valley and rummage for gravel then why should it not be transformed for people and wildlife after its industrial use has been fully exploited? So it transpired that on 15 January 2007 the trust made the biggest land purchase in its history, thanks to generous donations from members and an investment of £800,000 from the North West Development Agency and the Tubney Charitable Trust. The bold enterprise was ultimately to cost a total of £10 million, subsequently funded by the North West Development Agency, Natural England, Lancashire Environment Fund and the Tubney Charitable Trust.

In February 2008, the trust announced that Adam Khan Architects had been chosen for its inspirational design concept – a floating village comprising a cluster of buildings constructed of wood resembling an ancient marshland village. Work began on construction in December 2009, and it was floated for the first time in March 2011. The prestigious 106-acre Brockholes Nature Reserve was officially opened to the public by

A little grebe, also known as a dabchick, feeds its youngster at Brockholes. *Courtesy of Peter Smith.*

Brockholes Nature Reserve (Visitor Village centre). *Courtesy of Lancashire Wildlife Trust.*

the President of the Wildlife Trust, Simon King, on Easter Sunday 2011, as a high-value biodiversity asset appealing to school children, families and naturalists alike. In the early years, nature reserves were viewed as places where nature was protected not only from development but also from people. The Brockholes Reserve was designed from the outset as a place where people could feel free to explore nature – a notion reiterated by Anne Selby, Chief Executive Officer of the trust at the time of the opening: 'We are calling it the unreserved reserve because we want to bring nature to the forefront of people's minds in a way that they can both enjoy and feel free to explore. We hope this iconic reserve will emphasise the importance of our natural resources.'

Brockholes is situated at a strategic location in the river Ribble corridor, just upstream of the tidal stretch of the river at Church Deeps, Walton-le-Dale. Significantly, it connects with other wetland sites such as the Grimsargh and Alston wetlands, as well as ancient woodlands lining the Ribble Valley and areas of unimproved grasslands at Grange Park. The floating pontoon with its Visitor Village centre has been designed to cope with a floodplain environment and incorporates an education and interpretation centre, a shop, restaurant and conference facilities. A purpose-built classroom enables school children to encounter nature with the trust's team of environmental education experts. Significantly, it is envisaged that the transformation of what was once a brown-field site will act as a catalyst for social and environmental reform for the region.

The legacy of the local quarrying industry has left several meres which are excellent for waterfowl. There have been many species of bird recorded at Brockholes and careful management to attract all forms of wildlife including, for example, diminishing breeding populations of tree sparrow, skylark, lapwing, redshank and snipe, which provides optimism for the future. Increasing human pressures on their wintering areas in sub-Saharan Africa are thought to be partly responsible for the precipitous decline of many of our summer visitors, poignantly exemplified by the plight of the cuckoo. Nevertheless, Brockholes Reserve has the potential to be one of the richest wildlife sites in north-west England and is expected to attract a quarter of a million visitors a year. What remains of wild Britain now needs to be carefully preserved, so that the countryside may be enjoyed by everyone, and thankfully this conservation policy is being vigorously pursued at the newly created nature reserve of Brockholes. All of this is excellent news for wildlife and the public.

Walks commencing and finishing at Brockholes Nature Reserve/car park

The three walks described below cater for all abilities and are clearly indicated by colour-coded posts. In addition, the Ribble Way public footpath and combined Guild Wheel cycleway – where dogs may be taken – bisects the reserve. The blue (Reserve) and yellow (Gravel Pit) walks have been designed to incorporate hard-topped paths for wheelchair us-ers and pushchairs. The maps/flyers obtainable at the visitor centre give an estimate of the time that should be allowed but when birdwatching is in progress the walks can obviously take longer with frequent stops. So as a general rule allow at least half as much time again for each walk. All three walks commence at the Visitor Village and may, of course, be shortened or extended. Guided walks of the reserve are available throughout the year.

The Yellow Route (Gravel Pit Trail)

The first route is known as the Gravel Pit Trail or yellow route and is the shortest walk (800 metres from the car park or 1,300 metres from the Visitor Village), taking in habitat that has been developed as a microcosm of the whole reserve. With minimal stops the walk is likely to take about one hour.

It is hoped the improved wetland habitat will attract the rare water vole to Brockholes.
Courtesy of Peter Smith.

> *From the Visitor Village follow the yellow route through the car park and head north to the river Ribble. Ascend a gentle slope overlooking the Ribble to a viewpoint.*

During early spring vocal lapwings perform an unsurpassed tumbling display flight. These are magical birds that really capture the imagination, lift your spirit and take you back to the time when on warm summer evenings the sound of a snipe tumbling to earth with vibrating, spread tail-feathers produced a characteristic drumming sound, which sadly is no longer a part of the local scene and belies the name 'common' snipe. A principal objective will be to attract this species to the reserve by improving the habitat. At the time of writing the song of the skylark may still be enjoyed over suitable habitat at Brockholes and hopefully a population of this charismatic harbinger of spring will be sustained.

In winter look out for flocks of linnet and goldfinch feeding on the seed heads – appropriately the collective noun of the latter bird is a 'charm'. During October skeins of pink-footed geese arrive from Icelandic breeding grounds, to wintering grounds at Over Wyre and the Ribble – especially Martin Mere – and may occasionally be seen flying in a V-formation over the Brockholes Reserve. Local movements take place during the winter, usually as a result of disturbance on the feeding grounds, and evidence suggests they also follow a flight line along the Ribble Valley while en route to, or from, the east coast and traditional haunts in East Anglia.

The yellow-route path crosses a bridge spanning a small reed-fringed pool, which in summer is enriched with yellow iris, purple loosestrife and water lily; look for common blue butterflies feeding on the bird's-foot trefoil. Common lizards and certain amphibians, including common frog, toad and smooth newts, may be found here and elsewhere on the reserve. Reed and sedge warblers are starting to colonise the newly planted reeds and coot and moorhen nest, hidden in the marginal vegetation. The pool is also regularly patrolled by dragonflies such as the brown hawker, common darter and the emperor dragonfly. The rank grassland and marshy area is home to a few pairs of whitethroats and grasshopper warblers. The latter is an intriguing crepuscular species (active at dawn and dusk) and its distinctive reeling song should help to locate it at the top of a grassy tuft or partly concealed in a small bush. Other 'LBJs' (little brown jobs, a birder's euphemism for difficult species!), especially members of the warbler family, are best located by song and calls – an indispensable method of bird identification.

View the river Ribble and the valley from the viewpoint where the river flows with increased momentum on its serpent-like course towards Preston and the estuarine mud flats and marshes so characteristic of Southport and Lytham. In ecological, geomorphologic and visual terms it is still a very fine river, though here as elsewhere, the surrounding landscape has been dramatically transformed during the second half of the twentieth century,

Great crested grebe – a chick hitching a lift on mum's back. *Courtesy of Peter Smith.*

mainly due to the intensification of agriculture. Sadly, this has led to a loss of biodiversity, perhaps best exemplified by declining populations of many farmland birds both locally and nationally. Fortunately, within the reserve the intention is to create a diverse habitat and already this undertaking is beginning to bear fruit and is being professionally monitored.

From the viewpoint use binoculars to locate the significant ruined remains of Salmesbury Lower Hall which may be spied on the south bank of the river alongside a farm. Here it is not unusual to see soaring buzzards over the extensive woodlands of the valley. Kestrel and the fabulous barn owl may be seen occasionally quartering over rough ground and the embankments, whilst the nocturnal tawny owl is invariably confined to the adjacent woodlands.

The Pink Route (Meadow Trail)

A longer indicated pink route (1,690 metres) takes in more of the river Ribble. With minimal stops the walk is likely to take at least one hour.

At the Visitor Village turn right and ascend the wooden steps up the bank to the hill meadow. This elevation provides an opportunity to enjoy panoramic views of the Visitor Village and the adjacent Meadow Lake. An option is to carry straight on to the banks of the Ribble where a concessionary path follows the river downstream to a hide overlooking Meadow Lake.

Meadow Lake contains a series of small islands used by breeding wading birds such as little ringed plover, lapwing and redshank. The reed fringes host important breeding populations of reed warbler, sedge warbler and reed bunting, and elsewhere on the drier areas of mud and pebbles lapwing, little ring plover, moorhen and coot find suitable nesting sites. Also look out for the majestic great crested grebes that breed on several of the reserve's lakes and meres. The valley is on a migration route and in spring and late summer, a seasonal passage of green sandpiper, greenshank, dunlin, sanderling, knot, and black- and bar-tailed godwit are possibilities on both Meadow Lake and the adjacent wetlands. Migrating ospreys fishing the Ribble during spring and autumn and hobby falcons hunting dragonflies and swifts in late summer before they return to their winter quarters in Africa are an absolute delight to birders.

Here also is a crucial migratory resting and roosting site for the whimbrel which may be found while en route from their wintering quarters

Barn owls look somewhat ghostly when hunting at daybreak or during the twilight hours. *Courtesy of Peter Smith.*

in Africa to Shetland and Scandinavia during April and May. Only during late April and May do large numbers roost on the islands of Meadow Lake and hence it is known by country people as the 'May bird'. One of the best clues to identification of this small curlew-like bird is its repetitious call.

However, star billing is probably conferred by serious birders upon several very rare vagrants that have crossed the pond from North America, such as semi-palmated sandpiper, pectoral sandpiper, ring-billed gull and laughing gull, or indeed the spectacular spoonbill and glossy ibis from central Europe. During the spring of 2012 a red-necked phalarope was an added bonus for one day only and a first record for the reserve.

During the winter over a thousand starlings, mainly from Russia and Northern Europe, roost in the reed beds. Starlings fly swiftly and from all directions to their preferred roost site with fast wing beats followed by a glide. They are well known for performing their own spectacular aerial show by creating extraordinary shapes and patterns above the proposed roost site before settling in the reeds. They do this in the belief that there is safety in numbers, bearing in mind an attendant reception committee of sparrowhawk and possibly other raptors. As the sun sets, the secretive water rail may reveal itself from deep within the reed bed with a bizarre vocal descending screech.

Between October and March large numbers of surface feeding and diving ducks of various species occur on the lakes and meres, sifting the submerged vegetation and diving for small fish and invertebrates. These flocks are likely to comprise tufted duck, goosander, goldeneye, pochard, wigeon, mallard and teal. Flocks of teal typically feed around the edges of the mere making their lovely bell-like calls; they are in fact the smallest of all the duck species and almost half the size of the largest, the more familiar mallard. The scarce garganey is an appealing duck and an occasional visitor during spring and autumn. In its autumn eclipse plumage, however, it can be difficult to distinguish this species from the teal. Large flocks of coot, lapwing and smaller numbers of snipe, mute swan, Canada and greylag geese are also regular. Less common visitors such as whooper swan, common scoter, red-breasted merganser and scaup have all been recorded. An irregular visitor worth looking out for during early spring is the dainty little gull – easily confused, however, with the abundant black-headed gull.

During mid-March the wheatear is one of the first migrants to arrive back from Africa. This colourful passage migrant heralds the spring and its distinctive posture should be looked for around the edges of the meres or on open land, typically around the car parks or in short grass on the riverbanks. The bird is unmistakable specifically when it takes a short flight to the next perch to reveal a bright white rump, and makes a particularly welcome sight after a long, hard winter. Continuing along the trail and down through the hill meadow you will be surrounded, in summer, by a medley of colour and texture from wild flowers such as meadow vetchling, bush vetch, marsh thistle and foxglove. This area is humming with butterflies, hoverflies, bees and other invertebrates and it's worth listening for the chirruping of a small colony of tree sparrows which nest close by.

In the river you may see salmon and dace momentarily jumping out of the water and the spectacular banded demoiselles performing their

aerial dances. The river is a good place to rest awhile and perhaps have lunch. Sometimes heard during spring are the piping oystercatchers and the strident calls of redshank flying upstream to their Bowland breeding grounds. They also nest on the reserve. The most abundant breeding bird along the river is the sand martin which excavates holes in the sandy banks. The position of colonies varies from year to year depending on the erosion of the bank. They prefer a high vertical bank often with water below. With luck one may spot a kingfisher darting up and down, and coming to rest on the over-hanging branches that flank the river. It is also worth looking for goosanders that frequent this part of the river. Goosanders nest high up in large holes in trees and lead their sizeable families into the river. Alternatively, on hatching the youngsters simply jump out, hopefully onto a soft landing on water. Mallards can also be seen with their brood of ducklings. The most bizarre mammal sighting I have witnessed was that of a common (or harbour) seal swimming downstream towards Preston. At first glance I thought it was an otter but soon realised it was a seal. Nevertheless, the river is providing an increasingly attractive habitat for them. An environment survey carried out on the river Ribble during the summer of 2011 has shown that over the previous three years the number of otters increased by 44 per cent.

Opposite   Migrating osprey may be seen at Brockholes during spring and autumn. *Courtesy of Peter Smith.*

Common seal. *Author's collection.*

The Blue Route (Reserve Trail)

For the more adventurous the blue route is the longest (4,300 metres), taking in the entire reserve and a quite superb walk. With minimal stops the walk is likely to take at least two hours.

> *From the visitor centre follow the indicated blue route and turn right onto the Ribble Way passing the site of Higher Brockholes and Boilton Marsh. Ahead you turn left into Boilton Wood.*

The hedgerows flanking the Ribble Way footpath come alive in spring with the songs and calls of blackcap, whitethroat and lesser whitethroat, chaffinch, dunnock, and tree sparrow. Chaffinches start to 'warm up' in February with a hesitant rattle, before delivering the full trill with a terminal flourish, and dunnocks sing their wheezy little ditty of a song. The commonest resident finch to look out for here is the chaffinch, especially during the summer months. Other resident finches include the strikingly coloured bullfinch and equally so, the brightly coloured goldfinch and greenfinch.

In autumn the hedgerows glow with the berries of hawthorn, which in turn attract flocks of fieldfare and redwing from Scandinavia that vigorously criss-cross the river valley in loose mixed flocks relentlessly gorging themselves on the berry crop. Large flocks of both species arrive in early October and quickly settle to feed, with numbers gradually decreasing by the end of December. During March and April numbers again build up prior to their departure to distant northern climes.

The brambling is an interesting and attractive winter visitor, sometimes seen when large numbers irrupt from Scandinavian countries. Look out for their distinctive white rumps as they take flight along with the more familiar chaffinches. They will quickly return to the ground and allow you to admire their bright colours. The copses and hedgerows hold mistle thrush, song thrush, blackbird, chaffinch, titmice, greenfinch and robins. Robins are common and rigorously defend their territories along the hedgerows and woodland fringe throughout the year. The robin has been voted the nation's favourite bird on more than one occasion, which is not surprising because he is such a friendly little chap.

At the feeding stations keep an eye out for the tiny siskin among the larger greenfinches, especially during February and March. Many siskins in the UK at this time of year are of Scandinavian origin. Meanwhile, a copious supply of nuts fed to the resident blue, great, coal and long-tail tits at birdfeeding stations in turn provides bait for the increasing numbers of sparrowhawks which regularly patrol the area. This predator seems to be more common than the kestrel which still hovers over rough land looking for small voles and mice. Legislation and enlightenment over the last fifty years have brought about a return of some species of birds of prey to the Ribble Valley. The peregrine falcon can now once again be seen flying over the valley as they have done since time immemorial, for in all probability peregrines would have been no strangers to the knights of the ancient parish of Grimsargh-with-Brockholes.

We pass by a specially created wetland habitat known as Boilton Marsh, designed to attract and improve breeding productivity of several species of wader, especially lapwing, redshank, snipe and certain other diminishing species including skylark and curlew. One of the first signs of spring is the melodic song of the skylark or the bubbling quality of the curlew's repertoire that is both evocative and haunting, as it returns from the coast to more traditional upland breeding grounds. Approaching Boilton Wood and in exultation of the forthcoming breeding season, a mistle thrush proudly delivers its wild and somewhat fluty mournful song from the tops of the tallest trees in order to establish its territory and attract a mate.

Walk through the lower fringe of Boilton Wood until the path veers left and out into the open to the north of Nook Pool. Pass by Nook and Ribbleton pools, paralleling the M6 amidst vivid grassland to reach Island Hide which overlooks the largest lake on the reserve (No.1 Pit).

In April Boilton Wood is brought alive by a breathtaking carpet of bluebells. The wealth of woodland flowers cannot fail to impress, with delicate wood anemones, bright-yellow lesser celandines and the smell of wild garlic hanging in the air. The trees of the ancient woodlands are predominantly ash, sycamore, alder, wych elm, and some oak. The understorey consists of holly, hazel and other shrubs. There are several species of mammal, many species of bird, and quite a few interesting invertebrates. A selection of colourful butterflies may be seen in the hedgerows and on the fringes of these woodlands, including the peacock, small tortoiseshell and orange tip which are present from early spring. Also to be found is the rare white-letter hairstreak butterfly, which is on the wing in July and August, after the larvae have fed on the leaves and flowers of the diminishing wych elms. The speckled wood butterfly has recently expanded northwards and is now regular in the woodlands, where the supporting cast includes an impressive list of moths: the angle shades, the snout, mottled beauty, silver ground carpet, the twin-spot carpet, the barred straw, and the clouded magpie. The oak bush-cricket is a notable species associated with the woods. However, many invertebrate groups have not yet been properly surveyed so it is likely there will be many more.

One of the best ways to observe woodland birds is to sit quietly and comfortably and just listen and watch for movement in the trees, ideally before the buds have fully burst and the foliage has transformed the canopy into a deeper shade of green. The springtime repertoire of willow warbler, garden warbler, blackcap and chiffchaff is a joy to behold, while a bird that has consolidated its position throughout most of the Ribble Valley during the last fifty years is the ubiquitous nuthatch, a worthy addition and with lovely bright plumage. By contrast the frail and secretive treecreeper can easily be overlooked, creeping – as its name suggests – up the trunk and branches of trees in search of insects. The colourful jay may be seen and heard flying through the alder thickets, where siskins should be looked for, especially during the winter months.

Boilton Wood harbours bullfinch, several species of titmice, goldcrest – the smallest British bird – and the wren which is only marginally bigger. In winter it pays to sharpen your perceptions and enjoy discovering the secrets of Boilton Wood, which often appears deserted, until a mixed flock of tits appears and then the woods come alive with 'bird parties' moving through the tree canopy, quite possibly finding foraging easier as a team. But this is not Amazonia and here at Brockholes blue and great tits usually make up the bulk

Sparrowhawk with prey – an unfortunate sand martin. *Courtesy of Peter Smith.*

of the flock, though watch out for nuthatch and treecreeper tagging along with occasional great spotted woodpecker. If long-tailed tits are present they usually set a quicker pace and the flock moves quickly away. The path is ideal for watching the trees and scrub close by for further signs of life and there are clues to be gleaned in the repertoire of bird song and calls.

Look out for mammal footprints in the mud, or better still, snow. Ubiquitous grey squirrels from North America replaced the last of the red squirrel population in the valley about fifty years ago and this particular alien species should now be discouraged. Stoats and weasels are likely to turn up just about anywhere on the reserve; it is just a matter of being in the right place at the right time. Rustling and moving vegetation in the woods, however, may reveal a common shrew or bank vole or even a much larger roe deer, the latter now well distributed throughout Lancashire. A chance encounter with a fox or badger would be less likely, for both are essentially nocturnal.

Leaving the wood and passing Ribbleton and Nook pools is a good spot to observe dragonflies – brown and migrant hawkers and emperor dragonflies patrolling the edges and common blue damselflies launching themselves like tiny helicopters off the broad-leaved pondweed floating in the pool. The emperor dragonfly has also expanded its range northwards during the last two decades and this, the UK's largest dragonfly, may now be seen patrolling the pools from early June through to early September. Little grebes are present on the pools in small numbers throughout the year and during winter it may be possible to spot the secretive water rail in the aquatic vegetation. Listen out for its distinctive call, a sort of sudden, explosive onslaught of shrill squeals, diminishing in clarity to a faint terminal flourish. In summer the surrounding grassland is alive with purple loosestrife, common spotted and southern marsh orchids, meadow vetchling and bush vetch, all providing food for the array of insects that you can find in this area, particularly butterflies and moths such as the six-spot burnet moth with its fabulous blue-black velvet wings peppered with vivid pink spots.

The Island Hide overlooks No. 1 Pit created by the Lancashire Wildlife Trust to provide not only breeding areas for wading birds but also an attractive habitat for migrating waders. It has worked well and from May onwards the ground is positively alive with waders and their chicks, including lapwing, little ringed plover, ringed plover, redshank and oystercatcher, which all make a welcoming sight these days.

From Island Hide continue on the trail and turn left at the end along the blue route/Ribble Way footpath, walking under arches of ancient hawthorn bushes. As the vista opens up another hide (the Peninsula Hide) will give you a dif-

ferent view over the wader island. Towards the end of this trail you will come across the sand martin bank, an artificial wall constructed in 2011 and successfully used by 26 nesting pairs in the same year! Continue to a large gate on your right which will lead you back to the Visitor Village. After a modicum of refreshment you might then like to do the extended blue route taking in the river and Meadow Lake which broadly embraces the aforementioned yellow and pink routes.

A Concise History of Grimsargh-with-Brockholes

The history and natural history of the Ribble Valley is both significant and diverse. The Ribble is flanked by lowland pasture and extensive woodlands, an integrated habitat compatible with interesting wildlife, and the history of the Ribble Valley is equally fascinating. The 'Brockholes Story' begins with the primeval forests which covered most of Britain. Bronze Age artefacts discovered in the area have included a flint arrowhead and although no one can be sure of the dates of the first settlements these finds could be of the Neolithic period, from about 2500 to 1900 BC.

Several items of Roman material have been found hereabouts, including a bronze coin of a specific type issued by Emperor Antonin, found at Boilton Wood. In addition, three other Roman coins have been found in Red Scar Wood, with the course of the Roman road lying to the north of the reserve. In 1995, an archaeological evaluation by Lancaster University took place at Red Scar in advance of the then proposed development of the land. Four trenches were excavated across the line of the road shown on the Ordnance Survey map. The Roman road was found to be relatively well preserved, averaging almost nine metres wide and with a cambered surface composed of rounded stones and cobbles, with finer gravels acting as a capping layer.

The former township of Grimsargh-with-Brockholes has its origins in a Norse settlement and former agricultural manor and was mentioned in the Domesday Book. The Vikings' influence can be seen in the derivation of modern place names including Grimsargh. The suffix 'argh' or 'aerg' was probably an equivalent for a summer pasture camp, probably with a cluster of wooden huts used for the shelter of cattle in summer. The name 'grim' is derived from 'Grimr', a Norse person's name. It is therefore likely that the land of the Norse township would have been in pasture and this was the 'argh' or pasture of Grimr. The tiny hamlet of Brockholes was originally annexed to

Grimsargh but with the advent of local government reform was lost to the borough of Preston.

Evidence of the Scandinavian invaders became apparent in May 1840, when a great archaeological find was made at Cuerdale, close to the old Grimsargh-with-Brockholes parish boundary on the banks of the Ribble. The Cuerdale Hoard is one of the most significant finds of early Medieval silver ever discovered and is represented by an insignificant stone in a small hollow next to the river. The casket of buried silver treasure containing ingots and 10,000 coins, mainly of Scandinavian origin, was found by workmen digging drains. The items are early tenth century and probably belonged to the Danes when they were expelled from Dublin, the theory being that the treasure was either lost or left as a cache.

The *Victoria County History* summarises the documentary evidence for the origins of Brockholes, which originally incorporated the farmsteads of Higher and Lower Brockholes. According to the Lancashire Historic Landscape Characterisation programme (begun in 1999) the Brockholes site is classified as a 'Post-Medieval Enclosure'. An archaeological report undertaken by the Lancaster Archaeological Unit in 1993 on the site of Higher Brockholes revealed interesting data relating to the seventeenth-century farmhouse there, confirming that 'The site of Higher Brockholes now needs to be conserved and would probably benefit from modern geophysical surveys.'

A History of Samlesbury by R. Eaton (1936) provides several references to ways of crossing the Ribble by ford, ferry and bridge. On the river just above Samlesbury church a rowing-boat ferry was established, linking Samlesbury with Grimsargh-with-Brockholes at SD 59883500. It was served by two ferrymen in 1379 and continued in regular use until a wooden bridge was built in 1824. The boatmen lived near the ferry on the Samlesbury side. At the time of operation a footpath went slightly south-east from Higher Brockholes to the ferry then followed the riverbank.

Historical references to the flora of Brockholes in 1883 are contained in Dobson's *Rambles by the Ribble:*

> In the weed, by the wayside, there grows very plentifully and very luxu-
> riantly, the handsomest of the fern tribe, indigenous to these islands, the
> royal fern (Osmunda Regalis). In the same wood the clinging corydalis is
> very abundant, and is scarcely to be met with elsewhere in the district.
> The scarce carex pseudo cyperus grows in a ditch by the side of a wood
> near here, and the moneywort is very abundant upon a bank near Lower
> Brockholes. The hemp agrimony is not infrequent in wet places about
> the sides of the woods in both Higher and Lower Brockholes. The rare

broad-leaved ragwort grows by the Ribbleside beyond Red Scar and is reported also in some places higher up the stream. The whole valley about here is good ground for the botanist ... Until 1860 Ribbleton Moor was a swampy and desolate tract of land, to the east of Preston. The beautiful Marsh Gentian is recorded as having been abundant here and the Bog-beam scarcely less so.

That Victorian scene has long gone and several of the plants referred to, including the marsh gentian and royal fern, are now extinct in the area. During the 1960s, long before it became a nature reserve, I enjoyed walks at all times of the day around Brockholes and along the banks of the Ribble. At dawn Higher Brockholes Farm loomed out of the swirl of the Ribble's early morning mist. During hay time the scent of new-mown hay would waft on the air from the surrounding fields, and as the sun sank below the horizon the last occupants of Higher Brockholes revealed their presence. At twilight a pair of barn owls, also known as white or screech owls, emerged from within the derelict farmstead, ghostly and screaming, before flying off into the pitch black night to commence hunting.

Today only a lonesome pine tree at the side of the Ribble Way marks the site of Higher Brockholes and the curtilage thereof. Lonesome indeed for it has endured major transformation of the landscape of the Ribble Valley and would have many a tale to tell.

Opposite top   Higher Brockholes Farm nestling in the landscape of Grimsargh-with-Brockholes long before modernisation of the farming industry and Brockholes Nature Reserve. *Author's collection.*

Opposite bottom   A close up of Higher Brockholes Farm. *Author's Collection.*

Walking in the Footsteps of Cromwell
from Walton-le-Dale to Elston Lane
& on to Grimsargh

Start/finish	Start at the Shawes Arms, Walton-le-Dale; finish at the Plough Inn, Grimsargh
Grid Ref	550285
Distance	4.5 miles (7.2 kilometres)
Time	8 hours, depending on time spent at Brockholes Reserve
Grade	Easy apart from steep steps crossing the valley of Tun Brook
General	Refreshment and toilet facilities at Brockholes Reserve

The described walk is from Walton-le-Dale to Grimsargh incorporating the Ribble Way, Brockholes Nature Reserve (see previous walk) and Red Scar and Tun Brook, where extensive ancient woodlands flank the Ribble. We begin by focusing upon the historic significance of the lower Ribble Valley, which is closely associated with Oliver Cromwell and the Battle of Preston, a crucial battle of the Civil War fought on 17 August 1648 at Ribbleton Moor to the north-west of the Brockholes Reserve, before the fighting moved west to London Road at Walton-le-Dale.

Walking in the Footsteps of Cromwell

Before and after the Norman Conquest warring factions and explorers alike have negotiated the relatively gentle contours of Wharfedale and the Ribble Valley landscape as an east to west route. Cromwell was also quick to exploit

Opposite A male hawfinch. I have only rarely encountered this species in the Red Scar woodlands and it is probably now extinct in the area. *Courtesy of Maurice Jones.*

its strategic value in the Battle of Preston. This was probably the most crucial conflict of the Civil Wars, for few military actions have changed English history as dramatically as Oliver Cromwell's defeat of the Scottish army and the English northern royalists at Preston.

Preston in Amounderness was well known as a stronghold for the king's cause but there were also strong divisions in the town. The royalists of King Charles I were dubbed Cavaliers whilst Oliver Cromwell's parliamentarians were named Roundheads. The Scots supported Charles on the understanding that Presbyterianism should be the official religion in England. They promised to send an army to release Charles from imprisonment by parliament and restore him to the throne. General Cromwell was determined to stop their progress south, although the combined Scots and royalist forces easily outnumbered Cromwell's army. The Duke of Hamilton was in charge of a Scottish army of 10,000 and marched south to capture Manchester, a parliamentary stronghold. In Lancashire they were joined by an army of 3,000 English royalists led by

Eaves Brook Valley, Ribbleton, was the scene of the Battle of Preston fought on the 17 August 1648. *Author's collection.*

Sir Marmaduke Langdale, and later by Sir George Munroe, from Ireland, with over 2,000 troops.

Meanwhile Cromwell's army crossed over from eastern England into Lancashire's picturesque Hodder Valley and was met by Major General Lambert at Whalley. Following a council of war with Cromwell and his officers on 16 August 1648, it was decided to reach the Ribble's north bank and engage with the enemy to the east of Preston. According to traditional belief, Cromwell marched over the picturesque packhorse bridge – 'Cromwell's Bridge', spanning the Hodder at Hurst Green. Historians now think that Cromwell's already rain-soaked army would have also had to endure the crossing of a swollen river. On the pre-battle night Cromwell is reputed to have slept on a table whilst in full armour in the great hall at Stonyhurst College before rising early on 17 August and sending an advanced guard – known as a 'forlorn'. Contact with the enemy was first made at Longridge Chapel. Sir Marmaduke Langdale had his men firmly posted to stop the further progress of the parliamentary troops. Cromwell's officers commanded their men to halt and decided to keep the ground until reinforced with sufficient strength to cope with the enemy's advanced guard. General Cromwell was informed of the presence of the enemy, and he rode forward to the front to ascertain the correct situation and to remonstrate with his officers in command for not making an immediate charge. The general himself then ordered his men to march and the first blows in the Battle of Preston were struck. Cromwell's army was successful in driving Langdale and his men from their positions and they marched forward boldly to Ribbleton Moor, which at that time consisted of little more than a landmark windmill.

On the day of the battle Langdale had 4,000 men covering the eastern advance and messages were sent to the Duke of Hamilton that Cromwell was closing in on them from the north. Some time elapsed before the whole of the parliamentary forces arrived upon Ribbleton Moor, whereupon Cromwell's smaller force engaged with the enemy in the Eaves Brook Valley near where Grange Park and Brookfield housing estates are now situated. Langdale's forces fought back towards Preston to attempt to join up with the Scots but failed to prevent the enemy's approach to the vital river crossing at Walton-le-Dale. The parliamentarian contingent advanced along a lane which led into Fishwick Bottoms and the battle moved to the old bridge over the Ribble at Walton-le-Dale. The fighting was particularly severe at this crucial crossing of the Ribble, but Cromwell broke the enemy in two and the royalists were beaten back to the south side of the river and on to Wigan. Although outnumbered Cromwell defeated Hamilton's army, though he lost 500 of his men. About 1,000 supporters of the king were killed and 4,000 taken prisoner, before both sides ceased fighting and held counsels of war. Preston, one of the king's strongest Lancashire towns, had now been captured. Two days later most of the Scottish army surrendered at Warrington and Charles I and the Duke of Hamilton were subsequently executed. Today's modern London Road Bridge, which spans the Ribble and separates Preston from Walton-le-Dale, is next to the site of the bridge where Charles I's forces were defeated. However, this is an even older crossing and the very first wooden bridge to span the Ribble at this point dates back to the fourteenth century.

> *Commence the walk at the Shawes Arms public house, adjacent to the bridge over the river Ribble at Walton-le-Dale. Take the road next to the pub which now incorporates the Guild Wheel/Ribble Way. After a short distance turn left along a defined path leading to the wetland and woodland reserve of Throslack Wood. At the point where it reaches the Fishwick housing estate descend a narrow road on the right to the hamlet of Fishwick Bottoms. Turn left to rejoin the Guild Wheel and walk into Mellings Wood alongside the river. Continue past the golf course and under Halfpenny Bridge, carrying the busy A59 trunk road (a former turnpike and toll bridge). Continue to follow the Guild Wheel/ Ribble Way under the M6 flyover to reach Brockholes Nature Reserve. From here there is an opportunity to explore the new reserve before continuing along the combined Guild Wheel/Ribble Way through Boilton Wood and along the top of the escarpment of Red Scar Wood.*

The first section of the walk from Walton-le-Dale, via Fishwick Bottoms Nature Reserve to Brockholes Nature Reserve, follows part of the combined Ribble Way and Guild Wheel cycleway. The Guild Wheel is a new twenty-one mile cycleway/walkway around Preston, mostly off road, that links the city to the countryside. The walk through Fishwick Nature Reserve embraces different habitats of woodland, shallow pools, reed bed, gardens, agricultural fields with old fashioned hedgerows and the river Ribble. Not surprisingly, this is especially attractive to birds, mammals, amphibians and invertebrates including butterflies and moths. At least three specially made shallow pools have been created to attract orthoptera – dragonflies and damselflies. The interesting species which may now be observed include four-spotted chaser, black-tailed skimmer, common sympetrum and several species of hawker dragonfly, whilst amphibians are represented by great crested and smooth newt, common frog and common toad.

At Throslock and Mellings Wood a profusion of the differing shades of yellow lesser celandines and diminutive golden saxifrage awaken in spring

The nuthatch has expanded its range and is now quite common in the Ribble Valley.
Courtesy of Peter Smith.

to contrast with the refreshing blue shades of spring violets and delicate white petals of wood anemone and wood sorrel set in a blanket of sweet fragrant bluebells and white ramsons. Look for swathes of the lime-rich-soil-loving hart's tongue fern, a most untypical looking fern which flourishes on banks below the trees, where bright-yellow primroses burst open as true harbingers of spring. The colourful jay hides its acorns in caches throughout the woodlands and is not such a rogue as its larger corvid relatives. A chance sighting of a treecreeper attacking the bark of trees for insects or the puzzling calls represented by the varied repertoire of a colourful nuthatch all add to the intrigue and enjoyment of the day. Ubiquitous grey squirrels from North America replaced the last of the red squirrel population in the valley about fifty years ago and this particular alien species should now be discouraged. A selection of colourful butterflies may be seen on the fringes of these woodlands, including the locally uncommon brimstone, which are on the wing from March to May. Later in the season they are joined by red admiral, comma, speckled wood and sometimes migrant painted ladies.

On a day in late April it would not be unusual to see up to 35 species of bird. Likely suspects might include cormorant, goosander, magpie, jay, wood pigeon, mallard, goldeneye, Canada geese, mute swan, whooper swan, black-headed, herring, common, great and lesser black-backed gull, lawing/lapwing, redshank, oystercatcher, common sandpiper, kestrel, sparrowhawk, buzzard, mistle thrush, blackbird, song thrush, robin, chaffinch, curlew, pied wagtail, sand martin, swallow, blue, great, coal and long-tailed tit, treecreeper, wren, nuthatch, great spotted woodpecker, dunnock, house sparrow, chaffinch, goldfinch, bullfinch, greenfinch, reed warbler, garden warbler, whitethroat, lesser whitethroat, willow warbler and chiffchaff, to name but a few!

Moving on, in 1860 a new bridge was constructed over the river Ribble to carry the turnpike from Preston to Blackburn, replacing a wooden structure built in 1824. It was known as Ha'penny Bridge, being the amount of toll originally charged for pedestrians and traffic to cross. Today it lies closely alongside the busy M6/A59 Samlesbury interchange incorporating the motorway bridge that was built to span the Ribble at the time of the opening of Britain's first motorway, the Preston bypass in 1957.

After passing under under Ha'penny Bridge and the M6 flyover we reach Brockholes Nature Reserve (see page 47 for full description of reserve). Follow the Ribble Way footpath ascending through Boilton Wood and along the top of the adjacent woodlands of Red Scar and Tun Brook Site of Special Scientific Interest.

Throughout the seasons the Guild Wheel/Ribble Way footpath provides an interesting walk as we leave the Brockholes Reserve and ascend through woodlands to reach Red Scar and Tun Brook Woodlands SSSI. In springtime the woods are still clothed in the white blossom of the gean or wild cherry and give a fine display when walking up the valley. During the summer months the woodlands harbour numerous breeding birds including chiffchaff, willow warbler, blackcap, garden warbler, whitethroat, kestrel, tawny owl, treecreeper, nuthatch and woodpecker. There is an abundance of dead wood, ideal for woodpeckers, and all three British woodpeckers are known to occur here, excavating holes in dead or dying trees, often using the same tree for several years. The far-carrying laughing call of the green woodpecker is occasionally heard and provides a clue to locating this rather difficult species. This super, bright-coloured bird may be seen on the ground and fields around the woods searching for ants' nests and using its long tongue, specially equipped with sticky barbs, to facilitate the feeding. The great spotted woodpecker has a sharp 'tchick' call which is used for both contact and alarm. The great spotted woodpecker is the one that 'drums' regularly in spring and can often be located by following its range of mechanical and vocal tones. The easiest time to see both species of woodpecker is in spring, especially if rival males are staking their territorial claims, often accompanied by bouts of calling or drumming and chasing. Our third woodpecker, the diminutive lesser spotted, used to occur but has declined markedly in recent years and finding one would certainly rank as a red letter day. Similarly, Red Scar was once the haunt of the shy and illusive hawfinch but sadly I have not seen one for at least 15 years, though remain optimistic for you never know your luck whilst birding.

The old township name of Grimsargh-with-Brockholes contains a clear reference to its long association with badgers. For centuries they

The badger, or 'brock', has obvious connotations with Grimsargh-with-Brockholes. *Courtesy of Peter Smith.*

have lived in the wooded ravines of the Ribble Valley in harmony with titled landowners and successive generations of the farming community. A diverse assortment of mammals is present in the woodlands of Red Scar and should you want to see a badger you would need to organise yourself to do a dedicated badger watch close to a sett. Over the years I have enjoyed watching the nocturnal activities of these omnivorous members of the weasel family in the vast woodlands that skirt the Ribble.

Approaching the Preston Crematorium the Guild Wheel branches left. Follow this route through the wood next to the crematorium to read an interpretive board. Discover more about Red Scar mansion and the Cross family by taking the described short, circular walk.

Along the old coach road (Guild Wheel) with its towering avenue of lime trees great swathes of bluebells carpet the woodland hereabouts, where great spotted woodpeckers excavate their nest holes in ancient trees. What was Red Scar really like in its heyday? The site of the mansion has elements of mystery as well as charm, as it is bejewelled with ancient evergreen yew, ash, oak, striking copper beech trees and with its long-abandoned formal gardens in a park-like setting. A fragment of seventeenth-century pie-crusted pottery, discovered here in 2007, was donated to Preston's Harris Museum by the author, where it is now on display. A huge upright piece of concrete which once formed Colonel Cross's Observatory stands as a monumental folly and legacy to William Assheton Cross and the late Victorian era.

Red Scar & the Cross family

The Memorial Walk was founded by the author in tribute to three generations of the Cross family and the long-gone family seat of Red Scar mansion. Red Scar was originally built in the late-Jacobean architectural style incorporating a thatched cottage of cruck construction, on land owned by the Hoghton family, successive lords of the manor of Alston. The mansion was named after landslides on the steep woodland escarpment above the river Ribble, which revealed the red scars of clay. Hardwick described the scene standing upon the plateau overlooking Red Scar in 1857: 'No single picture can do justice to this beautiful and unique scrap of English scenery. The whole is not presentable on canvas from any one point of view. It contains, rather within itself, a complete portfolio of sketches. It is a place to ramble about in, and not simply to stand staring at; truly an Eden spot, fashioned by bounteous nature, to dispel the fierce burning passion and choking heart-ache engendered by rude collision with the outward world.' The steep inaccessible slopes Hardwick refers to have protected it from the pressures of agriculture and industries for many years.

During 1802 William Cross rode out to Red Scar and fell in love not only with the area and the view of the Ribble Valley, but also with a certain Ellen Chaffers, whom he married in 1813. The manor was subsequently sold to William Cross on 2 May 1803, for the sum of £630. William transformed the house into a mock timber and plaster Elizabethan-style mansion. The original thatched portion of the building was retained as the dining room, which was of cruck construction. The walls, on reaching a height of about 10 feet, curved inwards to meet in the centre to form a roof with the original oak beams breaking through the plasterwork. At one end was a beautifully carved altar with two wooden candlesticks. A door led to a small room behind the altar, which was very likely used as a retiring room for the preacher, and close by another door opened into a tiny pitch-black dungeon.

Ellen and William enjoyed marital bliss amidst the cherry blossom of the woodland estate and loved its beauty and purity. In correspondence to his friends William wrote 'that no man ever had a more happy marriage'. William continued to be absorbed in his work for the various churches and in political work for the town, but sadly, at the age of 56, he became ill and died on 4 June 1827. With the help of her three sisters and staff, Ellen carried on the work of the estate and the raising of her family of four sons and two daughters. She outlived her two daughters and saw her four sons grow to manhood. She died in 1849 and together with William her husband is buried nearby in the Chancel of St Michael's Church, Preston Road, Grimsargh.

Following William senior's death in 1827, his eldest son, William Ashetton Cross, succeeded his father as lord of the manor and married Katherine Matilda Winn. They had eight children. As Colonel William Cross he served in the Crimean War, and whilst at home he was interested in music – building himself an organ – and astronomy, having two observatories built at Red Scar where he installed some excellent scientific equipment and powerful telescopes. Day to day running of the estate saw him carrying out many improvements to the farms and implementing land drainage. He was a good and respected landlord and continued to buy farmland. William's brother, Richard Assheton Cross, was born at Red Scar and went on to become a politician of distinction and confidant to Queen Victoria. He represented Preston as a Conservative from 1857–1862 and later was returned as member for South West Lancashire, having defeated Mr Gladstone.

Red Scar mansion was the home of three generations of the Cross family.
Author's collection.

On the death of his eldest son, Thomas Richard, in 1873, Queen Victoria wrote to him: 'I cannot remain for a moment silent without expressing my heartfelt, deepest sympathy in this hour of terrible affliction. You know my dear Lord Cross, that I took you on as a kind and faithful friend and that therefore I do feel most truly for you. It is inexplicable that a young and most promising, useful life should have been cut off when he could have been of such use to his sorrowing family and his country.' Lord Cross became the first viscount Cross and between 1886 and 1892 he was Secretary of State for India.

The Cross family formed an intrinsic part of Preston's history, particularly as benefactors during the Cotton Famine and we are reminded of their legacy in the name of Cross Street, named after William. The story of the Cross family and Red Scar mansion can now be told with the Memorial Walk. An interpretative board is displayed at the start of the waymarked trail that passes through tranquil woodland and above the 'Horseshoe Bend' of the river Ribble and focuses on archaeological evidence of the former mansion and grounds together with important wildlife. A bench seat marks the site of the mansion, though the foundations are barely discernible. A huge upright piece of stone which once formed Colonel Cross's observatory may be seen from the Ribble Way footpath next to what is a now a serene and somewhat surreal woodland site where members of the Cross family once enjoyed an idyllic Victorian lifestyle with genteel walks in the countryside. Sadly, the mansion was abandoned (and subsequently demolished) in 1938 to make way for the huge Courtaulds Factory, while the crematorium opened its doors nearby on 25 January 1962.

Continue along the Ribble Way Walk skirting the top of the woodlands and passing through fields, eventually turning sharp right to cross over a stile into the wooded valley of Tun Brook. Cross the valley via numerous steep steps and a footbridge to emerge into a field; cross the field diagonally and over a stile onto Elston Lane.

This large upright stone is all that remains of Colonel William Assheton's Cross Observatory which was situated close to Red Scar mansion. *Author's collection.*

Resuming our main walk we cross the steep valley of Tun Brook, where in springtime the ground is covered with a medley of colours. There are great swathes of fragrant bluebells contrasting with the bitter smell of clumps of white ramsons. Elsewhere early purple orchids stand proudly and dog's mercury, enchanter's nightshade, lesser celandines, golden saxifrage, primroses, spring violets, wood anemone and wood sorrel are all to be found in early spring. Later in the season the greater bellflower and yellow archangel may still be found at the confluence of Tun Brook and the river Ribble. This latter species is at its most northerly range in Great Britain and there is also a clump of the rare green hellebore. The vanilla-like scent of sweet woodruff characterises ancient woodlands.

An impressive list of moths is also associated with the reserve: the angle shades, the snoute, mottled beauty, silver ground carpet, clouded magpie and barred straw are amongst those recorded. The oak bush cricket has also been recorded here. Emerging from the wood and walking across a large field, look out for whimbrel which traditionally occurs in adjacent fields to Elston Lane whilst on passage during April and May.

Whilst walking the full length of Elston Lane the refreshing aerial song of skylarks ascending and dropping like a stone and the yellow wagtail and yellowhammer are but a memory around Grimsargh. The latter used to sing from the hedgerows of Elston Lane a cheerful ditty, 'a little bit of bread and no cheese'. It is primarily modern agriculture practices which are the cause of serious decline of this once-common species, as the weeds upon whose seeds the bird depended to survive the winter have been all but eradicated. Meanwhile the yellow wagtail is virtually extinct as a breeding species in Lancashire, and the last vestiges of grey partridge, linnet, reed bunting, curlew and lapwing cling on. There is no better example of loss than the catastrophic decline of the corncrake from the fields of mainland Britain. A century ago this primitive bird was well established in the meadows of Grimsargh-with-Brockholes but has now retreated mainly to the Outer Hebrides. Nevertheless, in 1971 I was delighted to hear the rasping of a solitary corncrake from deep within a field above Gib Holme Wood at Elston.

Walk almost the full length of Elston Lane and after crossing over Tun Brook road bridge turn left into Elston Green (a cul-de-sac). Follow the extended footpath leading into Woodlands Grove and then left onto Preston Road to complete the walk at the Plough Inn, where a regular bus service serves both Longridge and Preston.

Opposite The coach road that led to Red Scar mansion (now part of the Guild Wheel). *Author's collection.*

The curlew still attempts to nest in the pasture areas of the Ribble Valley.
Courtesy of Peter Smith.

Entering Elston Green from Elston Lane, you are at what was once the site of Grimsargh Mill, situated at the northern extremity of Tun Brook SSSI. The corn mill, corn-drying kiln and large mill pond are all shown on the 1847 Ordnance Survey Map as being on the north bank of Tun Brook, a few metres downstream from Elston Lane and where the large wooden machinery was driven by the fast running waters of Tun Brook.

As the Victorian railway line through Grimsargh became more established after 1840, rows of terraced houses began to skirt Preston Road to meet the demands of an expanding population. These included Sunny Bank, Myrtle Bank, Kitchen Terrace and Longsight Terrace, all situated on what was then called Longsight Lane – now Preston Road. Demographics have changed a great deal in recent years and today Grimsargh, like so many other villages, is rapidly becoming a commuter zone for its city neighbours and farther afield, catering for a population of over 2,000 people.

The hamlet of Elston. *Author's collection.*

Haighton: from a Dun Cow to an Ancient Shrine

a circular walk via Squire Anderton's Wood

Start/finish	Start and finish at Cow Hill, Haighton
Grid Ref	574338
Distance	2.5 miles (4 kilometres)
Time	2–3 hours
Grade	Easy
General	Refreshment and toilet facilities available at Goosnargh and Grimsargh

Commence the walk at Cow Hill, Haighton, turning right along the drive leading to Clarkson's Fold Farm. Walk through the farmyard at Clarkson's Fold passing the historic outbuilding and follow the footpath into a field. Follow the waymarkers leading to Londonderry Bridge, spanning Savick Brook. Immediately after the bridge turn right and walk the footpath to reach a footbridge. Cross over the bridge and walk along the road through Squire Anderton's Wood. Exit the wood through a gate, taking the first farm drive on the right. Fork right and take a diversionary footpath past the farm that leads back onto the road. Walk ahead to the first T-junction and turn left to reach the ancient shrine at Ladywell. After visiting Ladywell carry straight on through woodland to Fernyhalgh Lane. Now retrace your steps back through Squire Anderton's Wood to Cow Hill and the starting point of the walk. N.B. at the time of writing there has been subsidence along the path at Haighton and a 100-metre diversion is in force.

Opposite This delightful footpath between Londonderry Bridge and Squire Anderton's Wood features part of the described Haighton walk. *Courtesy of Nellie Carbis.*

The Dun Cow story is well known in these parts. Legend has it that during one severe drought a dun cow was the only animal in the area still producing milk, and her efforts saved the local people from starvation. This, it was said, aroused the envy of a certain Pendle witch who milked the cow dry. The obliging bovine tried her best but eventually her strength failed and the poor cow died of grief and exhaustion. The witch returned to Pendle and the unfortunate animal was buried at Cow Hill. In *Traditions, Superstitions and Folklore* (1872) Charles Hardwick states: 'A locality is still pointed out, named 'Cow Hill' where gossips aver that, in relatively recent times, the huge bones of the said cow were disinterred.'

Meanwhile the relentless urban expansion of Preston east of Ribbleton has resulted in an inevitable loss of biodiversity. Land currently proposed for development still has roe deer, fox, badger and smaller mammals and a few familiar farmland birds including blackbird, song thrush, robin, swallow, chaffinch and less familiar species such as blackcap, chiffchaff, lesser and common whitethroat. The latter is fond of scrub with an abundance of overgrown hedgerows, where it may be seen and heard performing its protracted chattering flight song during April and May. Lapwing and curlew attempt to nest each year, usually with poor results, which rather symbolises the overall plight of farmland birds.

In Tudor times Grimsargh farming people were living in the farmsteads

The Tudor barn outbuilding at Clarkson's Fold Farm is Grade II listed. *Author's collection.*

A close up of the original cruck trusses at Clarkson's Fold. *Author's collection.*

of their medieval forefathers, like the present Grade II listed former house with integral barn and shippon, 30 metres north of Clarkson's Fold Farm at Cow Hill. The barn itself is private but a footpath passes alongside it. Nowadays it is used as an outbuilding, store and shippon for up to five cattle. Inside, three full cruck wooden trusses support the high pitched roof and gable. The house has an intermediate partition of timber framing and wattle and daub. Unfortunately the remains of the thatching have now been covered by a corrugated sheet.

Haighton House is situated in Haighton House Wood (known locally as Squire Anderton's Wood) and the house and immediate grounds are strictly private. In 1832 Squire James Francis Anderton and his wife Mary moved into the splendid Georgian mansion. In those days the wildlife of the estate was more prolific than it is today and during the shooting season of 1842 the squire bagged many species of game including 65 partridge and 74 brown hares. Several of the large family of 12 children suffered premature deaths, though this was not the case with Gertrude Anderton who went on to marry Robert Chadwick of the Hermitage at Grimsargh. The youngest child, Wilfrid Anderton (1844–1926), eventually succeeded his father in the

Nowadays the fox is a mammal widely distributed throughout Lancashire.
Courtesy of Peter Smith.

ancestral home as squire. Following the death of Squire Anderton in 1926 the family finally vacated the mansion. Fortunately a succession of owners has preserved the integrity of the building and woodlands. The wood itself is privately owned and maintained as a conservation area. To help protect the wood and its wildlife the owner asks that visitors keep to the roadway and refrain from picking wild flowers and dropping litter.

A good time to walk through Squire Anderton's Wood is at first light during late April when the dawn chorus brings a wide variety of birds to the listener's notice. How fortunate it is that one of our finest songsters, the blackbird, is also one of our commonest British birds. Chiffchaff, willow warbler and blackcap make a positive contribution to the chorus before these summer visitors get down to the serious business of raising a family. During and after dawn, warbler, treecreeper, nuthatch and great spotted woodpecker are likely to be active and with a little bit of luck grey wagtail and even kingfisher may be seen close to the meandering Savick Brook.

During late April the woodland is carpeted with bluebells and ramsons, providing contrasting aromas, and delightful orange-tip butterflies and speckled wood butterflies may also be seen. A pair of buzzards has taken up residence in the wood and doubtless preys on the local rabbit population.

On the mammal front listen out for the strident bark of a roe deer which may be seen in the woodland or at its edge, before darting away showing its conspicuous white rump patches. Nowadays this species is the most widespread of deer in Lancashire. Remember too that local foxes and badgers are both crepuscular/nocturnal, while typical diurnal mammals to be seen include brown hare, hedgehog and stoat.

Our Lady of Fernyhalgh and the Martyrs

Fernyhalgh is the diocesan shrine of Lancaster, embracing St Mary's Church and Ladywell House and its grounds, where the revered well and shrine is situated. On a ledge above the well is an oak statue of Our Lady holding the child Jesus in her arms. Fernyhalgh has nestled in secluded ancient woodlands for centuries as a tranquil gathering place for pilgrims from all over the world. The Chantries Act of 1547 resulted in the destruction of the small Roman Catholic chapel at Fernyhalgh which was probably in use from 1348 and into Tudor times. The Reformation brought about its destruction but it was rebuilt during the the time of James II, although the Vicar of Preston, Samuel Peploe (1667–1752), shared the general uneasiness regarding the popish leanings of the Stuart supporters and was very vigorous in combatting Roman Catholicism. There has never been an apparition at Fernyhalgh, though devotion to our Lady has meant that the shrine will always be a haven for prayer and spiritual renewal of all faiths.

This fieldfare is a winter visitor from Scandinavia. *Courtesy of Peter Smith.*

Above   Barclay locomotive No. 2 in the station yard at Whittingham.
Oil painting by Joseph O'Donnell.

Below   The Whittingham train leaving Grimsargh behind the antiquated ex-Southern
locomotive named *James Fryars*. *Courtesy of Alan Summerfield.*

Grimsargh Wetlands
& Forgotten Railways

Start/finish	Start and finish at the Plough Inn, Grimsargh
Grid Ref	584344
Distance	1.3 miles (2 kilometres)
Time	3–4 hours
Grade	Easy
General	Refreshment and toilet facilities at Grimsargh

Grimsargh village is familiar to many motorists and walkers who pass through it whilst en route to discover the delights of the Trough of Bowland and the picturesque villages nestling in the Ribble and Hodder valleys. Grimsargh might be described as the 'gateway to the Ribble Valley', for the view from Elston Lane reveals a picturesque river valley still largely unspoilt and rich in wildlife. Here are new treasures just waiting to be discovered, including the backcloth of the beautiful Forest of Bowland with its undulating fells and superb countryside. Grimsargh has a particularly interesting railway heritage and we begin this walk at the eighteenth-century Plough Inn which was originally Grimsargh Railway Station, before proceeding along the old track of the defunct Longridge branch line, an interesting part of Lancashire's social and railway history. Finally we visit the newly created Grimsargh wetlands, undoubtedly a superb birdwatching acquisition for Preston during guild year and hopefully for many years to come.

At the Plough Inn take the footpath immediately adjacent to the pub and walk in a north-easterly direction towards Longridge along the trackbed of the former Preston to Longridge Railway line. After a short distance take the footpath (right) that leads off right across two fields. Cross over a stile and onto the reservoir embankment, walk along the causeway leading onto Preston Road and thence return to the Plough Inn by walking along the main road (right).

The eighteenth-century Plough Inn has been a focus of village social life for many years and from 1840 it doubled up as the local railway station. Its walls have witnessed many comings and goings of local tradesmen, farmers and a succession of 'mine hosts'. Like many village pubs it has helped to characterise and shape the village. The inn was originally constructed in 1785 as a coaching house and combined farm, under the control of the squire until 1831. Landlords in those days had to deposit 10 golden guineas with the squire as an assurance that they would keep good behaviour at the inn. Another stipulation to be met was the provision of a loose box for a travelling stallion, and accommodation for the grooms. In Victorian times the landlords donned their second caps and went farming in the fields. Even inquests into sudden deaths were held regularly at the multi-purpose pub. The 1841 census shows Mary and William Walmsley as landlords, with six family members whose ages ranged from 4 to 24 years. In 1922 the landlord, Thomas Brown, was advertising the proximity of the railway station facility as well as 'refreshments, billiards, wines and spirits of the best quality, cyclists and picnic parties catered for'. Cyclists would perhaps have time for a quick cuppa before embarking on a voyage of discovery beyond the extremities of Grimsargh-with-Brockholes. Tom Brown managed the Plough as a free house before selling it to Matthew Brown of the Blackburn-based Lion Brewery. In the good old days before the large Blackburn breweries, horses and drays used to haul loads from the yard, for in addition to brewing their own alcoholic beverages, the Plough management supplied beer to hotels in Preston. In 1919 Joseph and Martha Walmsley and daughter Nell moved from Tarleton to take over the Plough. In the 1930s Ralph Ireland became the last village blacksmith and farrier to occupy premises next to the pub which latterly became the village garage.

Nearby on a raised embankment ran the Preston to Longridge Railway line, where we walk the trackbed whilst perhaps imagining the scene of yesteryear. The seven-mile-long branch line opened on 1 May 1840, as a means of conveying large blocks of ashlar stone quarried from Longridge, which was used to transform the town of Preston during the Victorian era. At first the only intermediate station on the railway served the village of Grimsargh, utilising the west side of the Plough Inn as a booking office. The fare from Preston to the Plough Inn was 4d. and to Longridge was 6d. Eight years before the age of steam, genuine equine 'horse-power' was the means of propulsion up the steeply graded route, and the railway company exploited the natural contours of the land by using gravity for part of the return journey. In June 1848 it was all change to steam traction and, thereafter, plumes of white smoke became a feature of the local landscape as the iron horse replaced the equine

Last passenger train at Grimsargh Station. David Billington bids farewell to stationmaster Lathom on 31 May 1930. *Author's collection.*

version. It was the coming of the railway in 1840 that facilitated the growth of Grimsargh as a linear village and offered a wider choice of employment. With the opening of a new Grimsargh Railway Station across the road in 1870, the former booking office was converted and the slotted shelves which used to hold railway tickets are today concealed beneath the plaster.

During 1889 a private railway station was built on a different site to the north of the level crossing gates (Preston Road) to serve the new Whittingham Asylum, and Grimsargh became a railway junction. The unique Grimsargh to Whittingham line (now dismantled) was constructed between 1887 and 1889 as a mineral line to convey coal and provisions to the new asylum. Hospital staff soon followed and private stations were built at either end of the almost two-mile-long (8,560 feet) standard gauge line. The Whittingham train, colloquially known as the 'nurses' special', once ranked as one of the most fascinating and antiquated Victorian steam railways in the country. Furthermore, it claimed to be the only free passenger railway in the world and anyone could travel as often as they liked. The line was well known to enthusiasts for its Victorian heritage and, long before the days of the Internet, the railway's inimitable characteristics were being acclaimed as far away as San Francisco, North America.

Thus who could resist boarding the train at Grimsargh's quaint branch line station for a free ride to Whittingham? On arrival there were plenty of opportunities to explore the landscaped hospital gardens and watch a local sporting fixture. Here was a community that seemed to have been lost in the mists of time, when the railway was the only contact with the outside world; when patients and staff began to discover that perhaps there was life beyond the gates of Whittingham after all! Throughout its 68 years the vintage locomotives and stock operating on the totally eccentric Whittingham Railway made the veteran steam locomotives on the neighbouring Longridge line look like today's equivalent of Eurostar.

The diminutive Barclay engines and unique Stroudley D1 – a refugee from the London, Brighton and South Coast Railway – that crossed over the level crossing in front of St Luke's main hospital building somehow completed the finishing touches and added to the allure of a remote establishment that seemed far apart from the twentieth century. Moreover, between the opening of the line in 1889 and complete closure in 1957 the tranquil railway scene between Grimsargh and Whittingham saw minimal change for almost seventy years. The extra freight and passenger traffic for Whittingham boosted returns on the Longridge line, with both lines enjoying their social and economic heyday during the first two decades of the twentieth century. Following the withdrawal of passenger trains to Longridge on 31 May 1930, freight and parcel traffic continued to operate from both Longridge and Grimsargh London, Midland and Scottish Railway (LMS) stations. The last freight train ran from Preston to Longridge on 3 November 1967. The Whittingham and Longridge lines symbolised the rural railways of bygone Lancashire with their quaint little trains trundling through a vanishing natural landscape embodying everything that was to be enjoyed about the Victorian steam railways.

Moving on from the railway, it was on a beautiful December day with the sun shining on the fells of Bowland and crisp hoarfrost adorning the trees and fields that I walked across the fields, whilst crushing tiny ice crystals under my feet, when suddenly a diminutive jack snipe flew up from my feet and I was left to ponder yet again over the mysteries of the migratory traits of passage migrants such as this. At the next port of call there is a goodly assortment of birds from far and near. I refer to Grimsargh wetlands, formerly a reservoir and the oldest of the

Stanier Class 5 No. 44874 on the Preston to Longridge branch line on the 2 August 1968 – the penultimate day of steam traction on British railways. *Author's collection.*

Grimsargh/Longridge complex of reservoirs built in 1835 to cater for Preston's expanding population, which doubled in the years from 1831 to 1851, from approximately 35,000 to 70,000 people. Progressive measures had included the provision of established water resources and Preston Waterworks was constituted by an Act of Parliament in 1832. On 1 November 1834, a contract was placed with a local stonemason – James Wilkie, of Preston – to undertake construction of two storage reservoirs at Grimsargh opposite the Grimsargh Mill at a cost of £1,600. A few years later the depth at Grimsargh was increased to 12 feet and a smaller reservoir was added at the eastern end. These additions increased the total storage to 53 million gallons and covered 21.94 acres. The construction of Grimsargh Reservoir and the coming of the first railway line changed the social fabric of the village in the mid-nineteenth century. Grimsargh Reservoir became an important water resource for Preston and in later years for the Courtaulds Factory, but following decommission in 1980 has ceased to have any operational function.

A public footpath crosses the causeway of the former reservoir, now an important Biological Heritage Site and potential local nature reserve to be enjoyed by the public. The creation of a new wetland for Lancashire by

Grimsargh Reservoir is now an important Biological Heritage Site for Lancashire.
Author's collection.

United Utilities is an exciting prospect for current and future generations. However, it would benefit from management by conservation organisations and mainstream funding to secure its long-term future. At present the wetlands are in an attractive state for wildlife and incorporate an especially interesting habitat – a mosaic of fen and open water complete with two islands, where several species of wader, mute swan, Canada goose, shelduck, mallard, waterhen and coot all breed successfully. Overall the habitat could be improved, for example with the propagation of a phragmites (common reed) bed and more shallow pools, thus providing a refuge for invertebrates, fish and amphibians, which in turn should attract animals higher up the food chain such as reed and sedge warblers, water rail and migratory marsh harriers. Rather than wait for natural colonisation to take place the transfer of rhizomes or seed dispersal could accelerate the ecological process.

Nevertheless, over 130 species of bird have been recorded including uncommon species such as black tern, slavonian and black-necked grebes, osprey, hobby, black-tailed godwit, whimbrel, ruff, greenshank, brent goose, snow goose, long-tailed duck, common scoter, scaup, ruddy shelduck, smew and even avocet. The flash of blue provided by a kingfisher is sometimes a delight to witness during the winter months, while during summer evenings vast numbers of swallows, swifts, sand martins and house martins fly relentlessly over the wetlands catching abundant insects. Canada geese are extremely vocal as they leave their reservoir roost and seek a quiet stretch of the Ribble for the day. Significantly the adoption of the wetlands as a roost site for migrating whimbrel led to numbers reaching a peak of 202 on 1 May 2010.

Unimproved grasslands on the embankments support a rare meadowland flora that is representative of a type of grassland under threat in Britain and is reflected by the recording of eighty species of wildflower. The wetlands provide habitat for several species of dragonfly including *Anax Imperator* and *Orthetrum Cancellatum*. The embankments also attract up to 14 species of butterfly. The smaller mammalian contingent comprises pygmy and common shrew and the wood mouse, which in turn provide prey for kestrels and barn owl. At dusk noctule bats fly over the

Long-tailed duck have visited the Grimsargh wetlands. *Courtesy of David Pye.*

banks and are joined by Daubenton's bats, skimming the surface of the water, and pippistrelle and long-eared bats. Also during the twilight hours foxes and hedgehogs are occasionally present. Amphibians including smooth newt, common frog and common toad occur and the endangered and specially protected great crested newt are also present.

Opposite   The sedge warbler is now established as a breeding species on Grimsargh wetlands. *Courtesy of Peter Smith.*

Below   Avocet have visited the Grimsargh wetlands. *Courtesy of Peter Smith.*

Walk A – Alston Wetlands

Start/finish	Start and finish at Alston church
Grid Ref	597348
Distance	Walk A: 2.5 miles (4 kilometres); Walk B: 1.5 miles (2.4 kilometres)
Time	Up to 5 hours for both walks (combined)
Grade	Easy
General	There is an option to combine walks 'A' and 'B' or to enjoy them as separate walks. Parking facilities close to Alston church; refreshment and toilet facilities at Grimsargh and Longridge

From the car park at Alston church take the minor lane behind the school north to Alston Lane, turning left to reach the White Bull pub on the main Preston to Longridge road. Walk towards Longridge (main-road footpath) and then turn right at the first junction into Pinfold Lane. After viewing the Alston wetlands turn right at the next junction and continue to the end of the lane. Take the footpath across fields leading to Manor House Farm, situated at the end of a minor lane serving several farms. Turn right along this lane onto Thorn Lane and the eventually right onto Alston Lane. Take the Defra upgraded foot-path (left) that leads back to Alston church and the starting point of the walk.

A country lane near Alston church – the starting point of this walk. *Author's collection.*

The lapwing is a charismatic but diminishing species throughout England and Wales.
Courtesy of Peter Smith.

Before focusing on the small wildlife reserve of Alston wetlands which has recently been created by United Utilities in association with the RSPB's Bowland Wader Project, it is perhaps thought-provoking to feature the landscape and farmsteads that existed long before that. The variable field patterns south of Longridge are a subject in their own right and are best read from aerial photographs and maps. There are significant survivals of ancient enclosure patterns in this region. Enclosure of land began in earnest in the sixteenth century and continued into the nineteenth century, and had a significant impact on the landscape, with hedgerows in the lowlands and stone walls bisecting the upland areas. These features further characterise the historic landscape, probably of AD 1400–1500 origin. These days current trends affecting agriculture do not bode well for the future of farmland birds in a green European monoculture largely devoid of wildlife.

Associated with the dominant dairy-farming industry of yesteryear are some interesting farms and old halls which are very much an attractive feature of the Ribble Valley. During the seventeenth century many older half-timbered farmsteads were replaced by new farms built of stone as finances allowed, though some survived and farming people continued to reside in the farmsteads of their medieval forefathers. One such example is Alston Old Hall which is now a sympathetically restored dwelling that is not open to the public. Expert opinion suggests certain features could be as ancient as around 1290, but beyond conjecture the restored farmhouse is a good example of medieval architecture.

Alston wetlands have been created on the site of the old Alston No. 3 Reservoir to provide suitable habitat for a range of wildlife, in particular breeding waders which are in sharp decline throughout the UK. The wetlands are a designated Biological Heritage Site and have recently benefited from funding from Natural England's Higher Level Stewardship Scheme. An electric fence encircling the site may help to deter animals that prey on ground-nesting birds. There are three viewing screens along Pinfold Lane that facilitate birdwatching at all times throughout the year, but the rest of the Alston Reservoir site, including the fields and reservoir banks, remains private.

The wetlands are acknowledged by ornithologists as a habitat for unusual passage migrants and breeding birds. Lapwing, redshank, oystercatcher, common sandpiper and little ring plover all breed here and require short cattle-grazed wet grassland, shallow open water and mud rich in invertebrates in order to raise their young. A free-design artificial sandbank has been built next to the main lagoon for sand martins and during 2011 it attracted a thriving colony with over 450 nesting burrows excavated by the breeding birds.

A brown hare typically seeking refuge in long grass. *Courtesy of Peter Smith.*

A sand martin colony has been established at Alston wetlands. *Courtesy of Peter Smith.*

The wetlands and remains of the old reservoir banks have considerable ecological and educational value, supporting a rare meadowland, ancient flora and being representative of a type of grassland under threat in Britain which has declined significantly in recent years. Here is one of the biggest colonies of delightful early purple orchids in Lancashire as well as a profusion of primroses and other associated meadowland flora. The endearing brown hare and the now widely distributed roe deer are both present, while the nationally scarce dragonfly, the red veined darter, was recorded here during 2009. Indeed there is a whole host of flora and fauna, including rare amphibians, bats, lepidoptera, odonata and birds, some of which are afforded special protection under the provisions of the Wildlife and Countryside Act, 1981. Furthermore, it is all there and just waiting to be discovered – enjoy!

Three redshanks and a dunlin (right). *Courtesy of Peter Smith.*

Walk B – Alston and the River Ribble

Drive or walk down Alston Lane (if continuing the extended walk), passing Alston Hall and descending a steep hill to a road junction. At the junction park off-road to commence a circular walk heading in the direction of a red-brick house and a pond on your right. Cross over a stile (right) and walk diagonally across a large field passing a depression/pond, whilst walking towards a wood that flanks the river Ribble. Take the concessionary riverside path and follow the path as it curves right to eventually reach a small copse at Alston Bottoms. From here leave the river by taking the track (right) that leads past several dwellings to the starting point of the walk.

The Alston river walk is one of my favoured local walks, especially on a pristine Christmas Day morning, ideally when the Bowland fells are carpeted with snow and a blanket of hoarfrost adorns the trees and hedgerows transforming the landscape into a magical Christmas wonderland – an

When birding check out characteristics. The photo below is of a grey heron but might have been something much rarer. *Courtesy of Peter Smith.*

The brambling is an interesting member of the finch family that can easily be overlooked. *Courtesy of Peter Smith.*

ideal escape route for a couple of hours, I think! On one such day I startled seven roe deer which promptly swam across the partly frozen river. Of course, all the seasons and times of day should be exploited and a very rare crepuscular heron was recorded on the river at dusk here a few years ago by two competent ornithologist friends of mine. I personally watched a migrating honey buzzard gliding on thermals over the valley in May 2008. At all times of the year, though, mallard, heron, buzzard, mute swan, great spotted woodpecker, nuthatch and kingfisher may readily be seen.

From the pastures in springtime comes the romantic sounds of courting curlew and lapwing, while overhead you can enjoy the welcoming sight of returning house martin, swallow and swift back from their long trans-Saharan flight from deepest Africa. The most abundant breeding bird along the river is the sand martin which excavates holes in the sandy banks. The position of colonies varies from year to year depending on the erosion of the banks, as they prefer a high vertical bank often with water below. Always a hive of activity, the best time to visit is probably the second half of April when the birds are busy creating their arm-long holes. Herons are commonly seen flying across the river and landing on the far bank to commence fishing in

Care should be taken not to confuse the otter with the alien mink, pictured here.
Courtesy of Peter Smith.

tranquil waters below the steep wooded escarpment of Jackson's Bank. That other avian expert at catching fish, the cormorant, has in recent years had to adapt from coastal waters to rivers, owing to a shortage of fish. Until fairly recently cormorants were regular along this stretch of the Ribble and goodly numbers roosted in several dead trees below Jackson's Bank. Sadly they have been charged with being in competition with man and consequently their numbers have been drastically reduced.

Of the wildfowl, mallard are the commonest, followed by goosander. Goosanders nest in holes in trees or special nest boxes. On hatching, their young simply jump out onto the water. As they grow, several broods can be amalgamated to form a crèche but by this time only the females are left, the males having undertaken a moult migration. Surprisingly, ringing has shown that many travel as far as Norway just to renew their feathers! During autumn and winter the resident goosander flocks are joined by other species of wildowl, which have included isolated occurrences of the uncommon smew, a member of the same family of sawbills. More usual are parties of goldeneye and sometimes whooper swans. Fieldfare, redwing and brambling also occur in the fields, hedgerows and copses, the latter species tending to frequent the tall beech trees situated where the end of Alston Lane meets the river, but may also be looked for on the ground feeding on beech mast with more usual flocks of chaffinch.

During the spring and summer months red admiral, small tortoiseshell, painted lady and peacock butterflies add a dash of colour along the riverbank, where the invasive Himalayan balsam is now prolific. There have been isolated reports of otter sightings along this stretch of the Ribble during recent years, which suggests that this hitherto rare mammal is gradually making a come back and that there are plentiful supplies of fish to sustain a population in an altogether cleaner environment. However, care should always be taken not to confuse the otter with the alien mink which is also present here and along many stretches of the Ribble.

The improved cleanliness of the rivers of Lancashire has meant that during autumn we can marvel at the sight of the salmon vaulting up the rapids or languishing in the calmer sections as they make their way up to the higher reaches of the river to spawn. Sea trout, trout, lamprey and a range of coarse fish are also present, thereby presenting a good challenge for fishermen, here evidenced by a photograph showing a good friend of mine, Richard Owen, with his salmon catch caught at Alston.

Happy the man – Richard with his prize salmon catch. *Courtesy of Kay Owen.*

The Best of Beacon Fell

Start/finish	Start and finish at Bowland Visitor Centre car park, Beacon Fell
Grid Ref	565246
Distance	1.6 miles (2.5 kilometres)
Time	2–3 hours
Grade	Easy
General	A one-way road runs around the fell. Parking, toilet and refreshment facilities at Bowland Visitor Centre where maps, books and details of walks may be obtained

This walk involves a circuit of the fell through the most productive habitat. At the visitor centre, collect a trail guide and from the centre follow the path to the south-eastern corner of the park and continue the trail by following the sign to 'The Tarn', then follow the road leading to Quarry Wood car park. At the upper car park, climb a few steps and follow the directions to the summit. From the summit descend towards the visitor centre and take the first track right through Dewpond Wood to the road. Cross over the road and stile to reach Spade Meadow, enjoying fine views of the Lancashire plain. Turn left, walking along the top of Spade Meadow with the fence on your left. After a short distance, on seeing the car park, return to the visitor centre.

Beacon Fell Country Park is an area of rough moorland and coniferous woodland covering 271 acres, situated at the heart of the Forest of Bowland; it was designated a country park in 1970. The fell rises to a height of 266 metres (873 feet) and is isolated from the western Bowland fells. The country park attracts approximately 230,000 visitors each year – a magnet for outdoor enthusiasts and walkers. Linger at the summit to admire the view across

Opposite top   On Beacon Fell willow warblers may be seen and heard especially during April and May. *Courtesy of Peter Smith.*

Opposite bottom   Lapwing with chicks. *Courtesy of Peter Smith.*

A young roe deer amidst pine cones – a characteristic mammal of Beacon Fell.
Author's collection.

the Fylde plain and the famous Blackpool Tower overlooking the Irish Sea. Close by, the alluring rounded tops of Parlick and Fairsnape trigger a desire to explore the rest of the Forest of Bowland Area of Outstanding Natural Beauty. To the south the idyllic countryside of the Ribble Valley is demarcated by the urban sprawl of Preston and south Lancashire, where to the south-east the television and radio masts clearly identify Winter Hill and the range of the West Pennine Moors. On days of exceptional visibility the mountains of North Wales and the distinct profile of Great Orme at Llandudno may be observed. To the north the unfolding panorama embraces the Lune estuary, Morecambe Bay and farther afield the Cumbrian fells, here dominated by the isolated splendour of the coastal mountain of Black Coombe. Beacon Fell is a nice place to be in the evening to witness the spectacle of the golden sun as it gradually sinks in the west. Historically, Winter Hill and Beacon Fell formed part of the original chain of beacons that was used as a method of communication long before the marvels of modern technology.

The diverse habitat on Beacon Fell includes open moorland, farmland, meadowland and an attractive tarn, which has been designated a Biological Heritage Site. The surrounding farm and moorland are the haunts of kestrel, curlew, pheasant, grey partridge, lapwing, meadow pipit, skylark and snipe. Whimbrel may be encountered in the outlying fields or while flying overhead calling, usually in early May. Rarities observed during the summer months have included the hobby, pursuing swallows over the rough pasture. Peregrine and short-eared owl are only occasional visitors to the country park. The tarn was created to provide a source of water for firefighting but is now a favoured wildlife area for birds like the tree pipit, and on quiet mornings or late in the evening, the shy roe deer. In summer try your luck at spotting dragonflies which can be difficult to identify without a good field guide. Up to 11 species of odonata (dragonfly and damselfly), including common hawker, brown hawker, southern hawker, four-spotted chaser and black darter, may be seen. Dragonflies have been on this planet a mere 200–300 million years, with their complex reproductive cycle, and should be given the opportunity to perpetuate the species at least a little longer!

On striking off for the summit keep an eye on the ground flora of heather, crowberry, cranberry and bilberry. Careful examination will reveal one or two surprises, including bog asphodel, common cow-wheat and sheepsbit. Mammals include, in descending size, roe deer, fox, brown hare, rabbit, stoat, weasel and bank vole, but in keeping with the habits of most mammals do not expect to see them all at once. Butterflies may comprise wall brown, red admiral, small heath, large skipper, large, small and green-veined white, meadow brown, orange tip and small tortoiseshell. In summer the common lizard may be seen on the sandy paths and adjacent woodpiles, where it is quite at home enjoying a spot of sunbathing!

The majority of the woodland, consisting of sitka spruce, larch and Scots pine, was planted during and after the war when the fell was used as a gathering ground for water supplies. Fortunately the long-term objective of the woodland management is to produce a predominantly broad-leaved woodland which is much more wildlife friendly. Management includes thinning the trees and as

The coal tit is a typical species to be found in the coniferous woodlands of Beacon Fell. *Courtesy of Peter Smith.*

A male crossbill feeding its hungry brood. The upper and lower mandible are, as its name suggests, crossed. *Courtesy of Peter Smith.*

areas are cleared regeneration is improved by a policy of planting native birch, alder, oak and other deciduous trees along with holly. This helps the woodland develop into a rich habitat for birds and the peripheral areas of the forest are the most productive. The period from mid-April to May provides an excellent opportunity to see a range of resident and spring migrants. The pines attract chaffinches, coal tits, goldcrests, treecreepers, pheasant and wood pigeon. Along the forest edge to the south-east corner of the plantation is a good location to see tree pipit, great spotted woodpecker and occasional green woodpecker, jay, bullfinch and sparrowhawk. Tree pipits are fine songsters and live up to their name by perching and parachuting down from the tops of trees with their attractive song flight. In spring there are several other summer visitors to be seen, including garden warbler, blackcap, chiffchaff, numerous willow warblers and occasionally the once familiar cuckoo.

Listen for the trill of lesser redpolls to detect a flock flying over the forest with bouncing flight and often with mixed flocks of siskin. Around the tarn and leading up to the summit the finch family is further represented by goldfinch, linnet, bullfinch, chaffinch and greenfinch. Blackbirds and song thrushes are complemented in winter by their Scandinavian counterparts, the redwing and fieldfare. During April and May the summit might yield a tree pipit on the woodland fringe or a flock of crossbills, which nest early in the year. Flocks have been seen throughout the year but the best time for sightings is winter or early spring during a 'crossbill invasion'. A good view of the brick-red male or yellow-green female reveals that the mandibles of its incredibly powerful bill are indeed crossed. This bizarre bill must be seen

A handsome male chaffinch (top) and female (bottom) at the nest. *Courtesy of Peter Smith.*

to be believed, especially while attacking pine cones – they are the perfect tool for the job.

The walk back to the visitor centre is through fairly dense coniferous woodland, with its canopy producing a subdued and rather sterile environment. It is therefore refreshing to complete the walk via Spade Meadow with its panoramic views of the Lancashire plain and coast. Spade Meadow forms part of an old and complex landscape. The history of the meadow shows that in 1885, at the time of a farm sale, it was enclosed in three or four fields, one of which was named Pure Meadow. Spade Meadow has managed to escape conversion to rye grass monoculture and remains relatively species-rich, which hopefully future management will encourage.

The colourful jay is a member of the crow family and is common on Beacon Fell. *Courtesy of Peter Smith.*

The Mythical Bleasdale Circle

Start/finish	Start and finish at Bleasdale Village Hall
Grid Ref	574454
Distance	3.1 miles (5 kilometres)
Time	3–4 hours
Grade	Easy
General	Strictly speaking permission should be obtained to drive along the access road leading to the hamlet of Bleasdale which is a private road/public footpath. Refreshments and toilet facilities at Chipping

From Bleasdale School commence walking north past St Eadmer's Church to Vicarage Farm (left), where, after a distance of one kilometre, a short diversionary path to the right accesses the Bleasdale Circle. After visiting the circle retrace your steps to Vicarage Farm and turn right along the road that becomes a Wyre countryside footpath. After a ford/footbridge ascend a gentle rise onto a minor road. Turn left and pass through Clough Head Wood to Brook Barn. Keep left at the junction at Brook Barn and pass through more woodland before crossing over the upper reaches of the river Brock at Brooks Barn. At this juncture a picturesque packhorse bridge on the left is well worth noting. Continue to follow the road back to the starting point at Bleasdale School. An optional extension of the walk is to pay a visit to the 'Ailsa Grove' bird hide. To visit the hide take a footpath left below the village hall which passes through a wood before diagonally crossing a field to the bird hide.

This attractive circular walk through the diverse countryside of Bleasdale successfully combines the major archaeological site of a Bronze Age stone

Opposite top   The Bleasdale Circle – a visit is quite a surreal experience.
Courtesy of Malcolm Greenhalgh.

Opposite bottom   A delightful portrait of Parlick Fell in the depths of winter.
Courtesy of Graham Wilkinson.

circle signifying thousands of years of human activity. This treasured site nestles amidst a landscape dominated by Fairsnape, Blindhurst Fell and Parlick, the latter cascading into the surrounding lowlands of the Bleasdale estate where a selection of the commoner birds of Bowland may be seen. The Bleasdale estate is heavily keepered and hence designed to be home to red-legged partridge and pheasant which are here in abundance. Significantly, the large field to the south of Bleasdale Circle and copse is the haunt of increasingly uncommon waders: lapwing, redshank, curlew and snipe. The Ailsa Grove birdwatching hide which is situated beside the approach road to Lower Fairsnape Farm welcomes visitors, provided birds are not disturbed.

The RSPB's Bowland Wader Project helps manage the habitat for lapwing, snipe, curlew and redshank. Drainage and so called agricultural improvement has caused serious decline of these beautiful birds and they are now absent from large areas of the British countryside. The Lapwing Recovery Project monitors their annual nesting successes and analyses the best conditions for the species to prosper. The farm participates in the Countryside Stewardship Scheme, which provides better conditions for Bowland's waders with the creation of shallow pools, grazing livestock maintaining the optimum short tussock grass that waders need for nesting and feeding, livestock exclusion when young birds are about, and meadows not being cut until late summer after young birds have left. Meanwhile inland nesting black and white oystercatchers, resplendent with their long red bill, are more widespread as they continue to expand their range along rivers and into the fields of Bowland.

The above is a commendable example of the farming industry working

An oystercatcher broods its clutch of eggs beside a Bowland river. *Courtesy of Peter Smith.*

A Bowland curlew; the long, curved bill is specially designed for its feeding requirements. *Courtesy of Peter Smith.*

in partnership with a conservation agency. Conservation of the fragile environment can only be achieved if people understand, value and respect it. Sadly, many politicians seem not to have this insight and human activities have been allowed to lead to species becoming critically endangered or extinct throughout the world. This tragic loss of particular species should be seen as an alarm call and must be a catalyst for extensive research and conservation programmes. Stewardship schemes will hopefully give more help to farmers to manage land in order to benefit wader populations, but surely a more sensitive national wildlife-friendly approach is called for. The European Union needs to redress the effects of the common agricultural policy that has indirectly led to this cataclysmic state of affairs and to a sterile environment throughout much of lowland England.

Leaving the remote hamlet of Bleasdale, nestling in a green oasis and comprising a few houses, a primary school, village hall and church, a sign directs you to the famous and enigmatic Bleasdale Circle site situated in a copse at the foot of the western end of Fairsnape Fell, as indeed it has done since the Bronze Age (2,200–2,800 BC). This prehistoric timber circle was first discovered in 1898 by Shadrack Jackson and Thomas Kellsall and was the first ditched timber enclosure surrounding a burial mound to be excavated in the UK. During 1935 the burial mound was again excavated revealing a grave holding two 20-cm urns containing charcoal and cremated

Semi-aquatic dippers may be found bobbing about on rocks in the river Brock.
Courtesy of Peter Smith.

bones. These vessels are said to be typical of the Bronze Age and are now on display in the Harris Museum, Preston, along with the remnants of the posts. The original wooden posts that formed the circle were found to be rotten and sadly had to be replaced with short concrete posts, which is how you see them today. Like Stonehenge there is a great deal of mystery concerning the origins and original purpose of the circle and one is left to wonder whether it was based on science or religion, and to speculate on the nature of the settlement all those years ago.

At Clough Head Wood the larch plantation and dominant under storey of rhododendron thickets are not very attractive for birds apart from the local pheasant population; nevertheless with a bit of luck the trill of the lesser redpoll may lead to a sighting of this tiny member of the finch family. In spring deciduous woodlands farther along the road harbour singing chiffchaff and blackcap.

The attractive grey wagtail may be seen on the river Brock. *Courtesy of Peter Smith.*

A tawny owl looking inquisitive! *Courtesy of Peter Smith.*

Pass through Clough Head Wood to reach Brook Barn, where the lane to the right leads to Bleasdale Tower, the estate mansion, formerly the home of the Victorian philanthropist William Garnett. At Brook Barn junction turn left along the lane which descends to a bridge over the river Brock where a dipper may be seen bobbing about on the rocks.

That little gem of a bird, the grey wagtail, complements the upper reaches of the river Brock at an obvious packhorse bridge which straddles the fast-flowing river a little upstream. This is a good example of a bridge just wide enough to carry a tired quadruped of days gone by. Note that the bridge was built with low sides so as not to impede the loads that would have been strapped either side of the animal.

Sampling the River Wyre

Start/finish	Start and finish at Scorton Picnic Site
Grid Ref	506504
Distance	1 mile (1.5 kilometres)
Time	1 hour
Grade	Easy
General	Toilet and refreshment facilities at Scorton village

From the picnic site car park, take the footpath on the east bank of the river and walk the short distance north to a bird hide overlooking a mere. Continue along the path, before veering off right through woodland and returning on a circular walk to the car park.

Before commencing this walk, check the bird feeders at the picnic site for great spotted woodpecker, chaffinch, siskin, nuthatch and titmice, for all are likely suspects, especially in winter. From the road bridge watch the river for typical birds associated with fast-flowing rivers like the river Wyre. During spring the liquid calls of common sandpipers flying low over the river may betray the presence of this charming small wader, and the riverside path provides more opportunites to see a selection of typical species, including dipper, kingfisher, pied and grey wagtail. The riverine woodlands harbour bullfinch, siskin, jay, several species of titmice, goldcrest (the smallest British bird) and the wren (only marginally bigger).

The intriguing thing about the wren is that it always seems to be on the go, skulking amidst the foliage like a little impish mouse in characteristic posture with upturned tail, at the same time posing to deliver intervals of song that resonate at all times of the day and throughout the seasons. The male tends to be hyperactive, building several elaborate domed nests for the female, who selects only one then adds feathers to the lining. The other

Opposite Nowadays the great spotted woodpecker is commonly seen on garden bird tables devouring nuts and fat balls. *Courtesy of Peter Smith.*

A handsome male bullfinch. *Courtesy of Peter Smith.*

nests are not always wasted, however, as the crafty polygamous males may play away from home and have a different mate in each! Another interesting characteristic is that in winter they have a tendency to roost communally. There is an incredible record of sixty wrens snuggling themselves together in one sleepover in a Norfolk nest box.

By contrast, the harsh rasping sound of jays shows where to look for a glance of their colourful plumage flying through the alder thickets, where lesser redpolls and siskins should be looked for, especially during the winter months. In this season, too, those Scandinavian thrushes, redwings and fieldfares, are active, moving down the valley in loose mixed flocks. In spring listen for willow warblers, blackcaps and garden warblers in the scrub. The pace is relaxed and from the bird hides you can observe coot, moorhen, mute swan, mallards and tufted duck. In the summertime check the surface for odonata and feast your eyes upon the superb peacock butterfly gracing the heads of knapweed. Moving on from the hide the track bisects an area of shallow pools. Snipe are frequent winter visitors and during winter it may be possible to spot the secretive water rail in the aquatic vegetation – listen out for its distinctive groaning call.

Birds of prey such as kestrel, sparrowhawk, peregrine and buzzard can be expected almost anywhere in this habitat close to Bowland. The buzzard, often known as 'the tourist's eagle', is now officially regarded as

120

A long-tailed tit carrying nesting material to its elaborate nest. *Courtesy of Peter Smith.*

the most abundant bird of prey in the UK and breeding takes place in most counties. Likewise, the largest member of the crow family, the raven, is now being seen more frequently in peripheral areas of the Forest of Bowland. Recognition of its distinct croaking call flying high above is an important aid to identification, together with its distinct flight profile. Ravens may be encountered anywhere on this walk.

A hungry young cuckoo awaits its foster parent. *Courtesy of Peter Smith.*

Walk A – The Long Ridge of Fells

Start/finish	Start and finish at Jeffrey Hill (on Longridge Fell)
Grid Ref	SD 639402
Distance	2.8 miles (4.5 kilometres)
Time	Allow 2–3 hours
Grade	Easy
General	Parking facilities at Jeffrey Hill. Nearest toilets and refreshment facilities at Longridge or Chipping

This walk commences at Jeffrey Hill car park, overlooking one of the finest view-points in Lancashire of the Vale of Chipping and the Bowland fells. A discerning observer of the landscape may trace the course of a Roman road that followed a route from Ribchester over Longridge Fell and on towards the Trough of Bowland. For the energetic, the walk may be extended by following a range of footpaths shown on the Ordnance Survey map.

Legend has it that Oliver Cromwell named Longridge after the long ridge of fells that he crossed over whilst en route to battle with the royalist army at Preston on 17 August 1648. In fact, the name was derived from the Old Norse 'Langrig' and mentioned as far back as 1554 as Longryche in Ribblechester – the name relating to its geographical position on the long ridge that stretches from Longridge to Kemple End, embracing Jeffrey Hill and beyond to the summit of the fell at 'Spire Point', 350 metres (1,150 feet) above sea level. Longridge was originally made up of two townships – Alston and Dilworth – and it was not until the nineteenth century that the expanding village on its lower slopes was officially named Longridge.

From Jeffrey Hill car park, turn left up the road for about 200 metres. Look for a gate in the wall on the left, opposite the beginning of a plantation, and enter the open fell by ascending the footpath (which can be boggy in places) to the triangulation point of Spire Hill.

Opposite Lesser redpoll may be observed in conifer plantations on Longridge Fell. *Courtesy of Peter Smith.*

From the trig point take time to admire the view and then retrace your steps along the main path. After a second stile on the left, where the plantation meets the open fell, take the footpath (right) and return to the car park by following this attractive footpath along the side of the fell back to the car park.

On the rushy fellside there are still a few skylark, and also meadow pipit, reed bunting, linnet, the odd snipe and curlew. Buzzard sightings are increasing as this species expands its range from central Bowland. This is a good area to scan the moor for kestrels and the occasional peregrine, goshawk and merlin, the latter three species of raptor using the outlying fell for hunting forays. The nocturnal long-eared owl is probably still present in very low numbers and has had mixed breeding success over the years. It may also be possible to spot a diurnal hunting short-eared owl quartering the fell. Sightings of red grouse are still fairly regular on the slopes, although they have declined in recent years. The heather moor is also the haunt of curlew, meadow pipit

Kestrel with typical prey – a small mammal. *Courtesy of Peter Smith.*

The classic view from Longridge Fell must rank as one of the finest in England.
Courtesy of Graham Wilkinson.

and stonechat, while the plantations house lesser redpoll, siskin, bullfinch, chaffinch, song thrush, great spotted woodpecker, willow warbler and magpie. Nowadays, whinchat and cuckoo are less common summer visitors to Longridge Fell and unfortunately this is mirrored elsewhere in Bowland.

Among the spring and summer lepidoptera to be seen on the fell are green hairstreak, red admiral, painted lady, emperor and northern oak eggar moth. On reaching the trig point find a comfortable spot to sit down in the heather and admire the view, for there is no viewpoint quite so good as this. An added bonus might be the evocative song of the curlew calling from down below in the valley, or the perfect rendition of 'go-back, go-back, go-back' of the red grouse standing amongst the heather. This seems to be a particularly apt response to hunters.

From the trig point the pristine and ancient landscape in the valley embraces a mosaic of lowland pasture and a patchwork of irregularly

125

A view of Longridge Fell with Chipping Moss in the foreground.
Courtesy of Graham Wilkinson.

shaped fields, relieved only by an intricate network of roads, farms and villages and enhanced by the backcloth of the Bowland fells. On fine mornings with clear visibility it is a joy at any time of the year to witness the rising sun spotlighting the detail and features of Beacon Fell, Bleasdale, Parlick, Fairsnape to the west – not to mention Blackpool Tower – and Wolf Fell, Saddle Fell, Burnslack, Fair Oak Fell and the long expanse of Totridge to the east. With binoculars one can detect the Hodder Valley where the Trough of Bowland threads its way through the landscape and beyond the hills of Yorkshire. In moments of quiet contemplation think of the Roman legionnaires heading north over the fell from Ribchester along the Roman road into the Hodder Valley near Doeford Bridge, thence towards the Trough of Bowland and on to forts at Borrow Bridge, Penrith and Carlisle.

On the morning of 17 August 1648, Oliver Cromwell and his army passed over Thornley Fell and admired the view over the vale of Chipping, before engaging in the Battle of Preston. Hewitson in his *History of Preston* states that Cromwell is supposed to have said, 'I have seen no part of the country so beautiful as this'. On a nice spring morning one might reflect on this statement while enjoying the birdwatching in a superb setting enhanced by the overall atmosphere of this grand Lancashire beauty spot.

Walk B – Longridge Fell Woodlands

Start/finish	Start and finish at Clitheroe Old Road, south of Longridge Fell
Grid Ref	657394
Distance	3.7 miles (6 kilometres)
Time	2–3 hours
Grade	Easy
General	Refreshment and toilet facilities available at Hurst Green and Longridge. The privately owned woodlands are managed for timber production and areas of woodland may be closed during times of tree felling

There are many options to consider when setting forth into woodland at Brownslow, along numerous forest tracks and footpaths. The walk described below has been chosen because of the varied habitat it offers, which in turn is likely to attract a broader range of wildlife. Furthermore, the circular route affords excellent views of the surrounding countryside to the north and south of Longridge Fell. Throughout this walk it is easy to see why Longridge is regarded as the gateway to the Forest of Bowland and the Ribble Valley. On the south side of the fell there are extensive views of the Ribble Valley across to Winter Hill with its towering assortment of television and communication masts overlooking the south Lancashire plains. To the north is the Hodder Valley with its delightful river snaking down to its confluence with the Ribble at Hurst Green.

To reach the starting point drive along the Clitheroe Old Road from Longridge that crosses over the southern flanks of Longridge Fell to crossroads at the Newdrop Inn. Carry straight on at the Newdrop for a distance of approximately two miles and park off the road (limited parking) at the entrance to a gated forest track on the left. Walk back along the main road towards Lon-

Opposite Winter wonderland. Bowland is given a blanket of snow.
Courtesy of Malcolm Greenhalgh.

Pendle Hill from Kemple End, Longridge Fell. *Courtesy of Nellie Carbis.*

gridge as far as a minor lane leading up onto the fell (right), indicated by the sign 'Dutton Dog Boarding Kennels'. Walk up this lane and where it veers right to the dog kennels, carry straight on along a rough track onto the heather-covered slopes of the fell. On reaching a larch plantation turn left and follow the edge of the plantation round to cross over a wall stile. Turn right on the main track to reach the white trig point and then retrace your steps to the first wall stile (left). Cross over the stile and immediately thereafter fork left and follow the path that leads onto a forest track. Continue along this track to the first junction and then turn right, eventually reaching the main road. Turn right and walk back along the road towards Longridge to reach the starting point of the walk.

The redwing is a winter visitor from Scandinavia, often seen with fieldfares.
Courtesy of Peter Smith.

The forest clearing near the Clitheroe road hosted a handsome, and uncommon, great grey shrike during the spring of 2012. This grey and black individual medium-sized passerine featured prominently in the 'must see' agenda of many birders. However, a sighting was not guaranteed as the bird probably mainly frequented alternative sites. It just goes to show though, that the more unusual species should always be looked for whilst birding, even in what is essentially an alien commercial forest environment. More typically, fieldfare and redwing are to be found in winter and flocks of chaffinch should be checked for any white rumps to identify bramblings, which occasionally integrate with chaffinch flocks, especially where there are isolated stands of beech mixed in with the dominant conifers.

Evergreen woodlands are the haunt of three typically coniferous specialists – siskin, lesser redpoll and crossbill. The siskin and lesser redpoll are small members of the finch family that often flock together during the winter. During some winters flocks of crossbill erupt into the plantations and their distinctive 'chip-chip' note allows instant recognition. On the side of the fell and open heather moorland near the summit at Spire Hill look out for stonechat. The stonechat is a species that has benefited from a long run of mild winters but overall its status is subject to change as it can be severely hit by a harsh winter. The distinctive calls of red grouse and curlew blending with the song flight of skylarks, bubbling notes of curlews and staccato bark of roe deer enliven the moor and add to the allure of the vista below of the beautiful vale of Chipping.

A jay pauses amidst the woodland flora. *Courtesy of Peter Smith.*

A few broad-leaved trees and mountain ash laden with berries in autumn make a pretty sight whilst providing some relief from the innumerable rows of conifers. During spring and summer the forest is the haunt of numerous willow warbler, chiffchaff, blackcap, meadow pipit, coal tit, great tit, jay, raven, cuckoo, lesser redpoll, goldfinch, robin and nuthatch. In spring, whilst walking through the newly planted plantations, also listen out for the beautiful song of the tree pipit. Scattered trees and woodland margins are the preferred haunt of this declining species. It may be seen performing its vocal aerial display and parachuting down from a tree or wire in springtime, a feature which helps to distinguish it from the very similar, though more abundant, meadow pipit.

Returning towards the Clitheroe road along the forest track, view the upper reaches of the Ribble Valley (through binoculars) across the felled areas to catch a glimpse of the famous Whalley Viaduct with its familiar red-brick arches. The Blackburn to Hellifield line survives as the longest brick viaduct in Lancashire. It is 679 yards in length and 70 feet in height above the river Calder, constructed with 7,000,000 bricks, 436,000 cubic feet of stone, 10,000 feet of timber and 48 arches – and all for only £40,000, which even included a free silver spade and mahogany wheelbarrow for the first sod cutter himself, Lord Ribblesdale! However, the effort was not without human cost, for during construction a total of seven men lost their lives. Nearby Calderstones Mental Hospital was built in the Lancashire countryside in 1907 and was linked to the Hellifield line by a half-mile long private hospital railway.

The Chipping Circular

Start/finish	Start and finish at Talbot Street, Chipping
Grid Ref	623433
Distance	3.7 miles (6 kilometres)
Time	3–4 hours
Grade	Easy
General	Toilets, refreshments and parking facilities at Chipping and a regular bus service from Preston

From Talbot Street, Chipping, go past the Tillotsons Arms, left at the war memorial, past the Lodge House and concessionary path next to the road. Proceed left up Leagram Hall drive, passing Chipping Lawn Farm, and turn right at the fork to Park Gate. Immediately after the bridge take the footpath that leads to the North Lancashire Bridleway. Go through the gate at the top of the rise and onto 'access land'. Thereafter maintain higher elevation at the side of the stream until reaching the bridleway. Turn right along the well-defined bridleway to reach Lickhurst Farm, then right at the farm proceeding past both Higher and Lower Lickhurst farms. Keep right and follow waymarkers/stiles to a quarry at Knott Hill. Turn right by an old lime kiln and after passing the quarry veer left across the field to go over a stile by a gate in the far fence. Descend to a stream and cross over the footbridge. Follow the fence and hedge on your right along the waymarked path to reach Leagram Hall drive and back to Chipping.

This circular walk provides good opportunities to observe Bowland's precious population of breeding waders whilst enjoying their extensive repertoire. We commence the walk at the picturesque village of Chipping with its narrow streets and terraced houses, rich in character and steeped in history – the name Chipping derives from the Anglo Saxon term for a market and is an indicator of the origins of the settlement. Leaving

Opposite top Windy Street, Chipping. *Courtesy of Graham Wilkinson.*

Opposite bottom St Bartholomew's Church, Chipping. *Courtesy of Graham Wilkinson.*

135

the car park pass by St Bartholomew's Church, complete with ancient fabric and imposing tower dating back to the fifteenth century. Walk past the allegedly haunted Sun Inn and downhill past seventeenth-century cottages, including the village shop, said to be the oldest in the country with a history of continuous trading, and past the cottage where John Brabin was born. It was John Brabin who founded the extant village school on Windy Street, distinguished by its impressive studded front door and dated 1668. Cross over Chipping Brook Bridge and glance up and down the fast-flowing stream for possible sightings of both grey wagtail and dipper, at the same time noting the small rookery close by. Moving on past the lodge to Leagram Hall, it is interesting to note that during the reign of Elizabeth I this ancient deer park was the seat of the Sherburns who occupied a timber-built thatched wattle and daube building. Leagram Hall was rebuilt by their descendants, the Welds, in the eighteenth century and demolished in the 1950s, and its successor is occupied by the Weld family. The extensive medieval deer park of the mid-fourteenth century was bounded by a bank about nine miles in length and a ditch with a high fence to keep the deer confined. Today the deer have been replaced by a magnificent herd of a rare breed of white cattle. Flocks of jackdaw are ever present and the beautiful ancient oaks typically attract mistle thrush and a range of other common birds. At Park Gate survey the small plantation and waterfall from the bridge crossing over Leagram Brook, in what is a delightful setting for seeing a selection of the 'usual suspects' including grey wagtail.

Ascending onto the lower fells the character of the land changes and here wet grassland and unimproved rough pasture provide opportunities to witness curlews engaged in their wonderful bubbling territorial display, while charismatic, tumbling lapwings call 'peerrweet-weet-weet' (hence the old names peewit or tewit). Sadly, the lapwing is now red-listed as a species of high conservation concern throughout Britain. The ongoing loss of farmland birds cannot be blamed on the farming community; in fact there are many farmers who work closely with the RSPB to ensure that the industry continues to improve habitat for a diverse range of wildlife.

In the breeding season lapwings need a range of habitats to rear their chicks successfully. Agricultural intensification on pasture has meant increased drainage and the use of agrochemicals, resulting in much arable land becoming unsuitable because the grass is too high. On the lower slopes of the Leagram estate commendable efforts are being made by the Stott family of New Lawn Farm to buck the national trend of dramatic declines of lapwing and other waders by improving the habitat, with the inclusion of several newly created wet areas for lapwing chicks to feed. The Forest of Bowland AONB has the highest density of breeding lapwing and curlews in England. Oystercatchers have now taken to the fields as well as the river to join nesting lapwing and curlew, whilst snipe can still be heard drumming and delivering their 'chip-chip' song on walls and fence posts in certain areas of managed habitat. Other species that may be seen on the lower fells include skylark, meadow pipit, wheatear, stonechat, kestrel

An early hand-coloured photograph of a lapwing taken in the Ribble Valley when the species was much more common than it is today. *Watercolour by Norman Duerden, FRSA.*

Chipping Brook and the watermill, which became the Waterwheel Restaurant and is now a private dwelling. *Courtesy of Alan Wilding.*

and short-eared owl. Elsewhere the picture is not so rosy as farmers have been under increasing financial pressure to adopt intensive agricultural practices.

Moving on, redstarts and cuckoo may be located during late April in Hell Clough, where fairly sparse woodland extends up the side of Fair Oak Fell. After passing by the two farms at Lickhurst, the attractive tree-lined path provides an opportunity to look and listen for redstarts flitting about the fresh green foliage of springtime. Along the hedgerows and copses close to Leagram Brook listen out for the repetitive rattle of the lesser whitethroat, or melodic tones of the garden warbler, which provide an opportunity to see these normally skulking warblers. Also hereabouts, lesser redpolls feed on the emerging buds while parties of blue, great and long-tail tits may make their presence known in a wandering bird party feeding in the tops of trees. The latter species continues to prosper throughout Bowland in all suitable places.

View of the Bowland Fells from the North Lancashire Bridleway (above Lickhurst Farm). *Author's collection.*

Walking the Ribble Way:
from Mitton to Clitheroe to Chatburn

Start/finish	Start at Aspinall Arms, Great Mitton; finish either at Edisford Bridge, Clitheroe or Chatburn
	Alternatively start at Edisford Bridge and finish at Chatburn
Grid Ref	Great Mitton: 715388
	Edisford Bridge: 726414
Distance	Approximately 6.2 miles (10 kilometres) for complete walk
Time	5–6 hours
Grade	Easy
General	Parking, toilet and refreshment facilities at Mitton, Edisford Bridge, Clitheroe and Chatburn

This walk follows the south bank of the river Ribble along the Ribble Way from Mitton to Edisford Bridge, Clitheroe and/or a continuation from Edisford Bridge to Chatburn – the choice is yours. The complete walk takes in contrasting parts of the river. Walking alongside the picturesque riverbanks enriches the soul and the wildlife turns a pleasant day into a memorable one.

From the Aspinall Arms at Mitton, cross over the Ribble road bridge, turn immediately left and follow the indicated Ribble Way logo. Walk diagonally uphill across a field before descending and walking the riverbank in the direction of Clitheroe. Pass the distinctive architectural lines of the aqueduct carrying piped water from Haweswater and proceed to reach Shuttleworth Farm. Thereafter walk along a minor road and after passing a household recycling centre and wood leave the road and follow the Ribble Way logo left along the footpath to reach Edisford Bridge. Nearby Clitheroe town centre is a pleasant place to have a wander along the main street and into the castle grounds.

Opposite Clitheroe Castle dominates the town. *Courtesy of Malcolm Greenhalgh.*

141

A view of Clitheroe centre from the castle grounds. *Courtesy of Nellie Carbis.*

The second part of the walk commences at Clitheroe swimming baths next to Edisford Bridge and follows the course of the Ribble Way to Chatburn. After passing through the outskirts of Clitheroe at Low Moor and some allotments, Brungerley Bridge is reached carrying the road from Clitheroe to Waddington. After leaving the bridge stay on the south side of the river and fork left below Brungerley Park, staying on the upper tarmac path before descending a wooded slope to reach the Lancashire Wildlife Trust Reserve of Salthill Quarry, an important geological and botanical site. From here the path closely follows the riverbank to Bradford Bridge. Continue to follow the Ribble Way on the south bank, ascending a slope to reach the main road running from Chatburn to Grindleton. Turn right along a concessionary path to reach the village of Chatburn, which is adequately served by regular bus services to Clitheroe and other destinations (change at Clitheroe for Mitton).

We commence at the village of Mitton, the name of which is derived from 'mythe', meaning a junction of rivers, as the confluence of the Ribble and Hodder is only about a mile away. The village of Mitton straddles the Ribble and actually comprises the hamlets of Great Mitton on the Longridge side and Little Mitton on the Whalley side. The recently restored medieval church of All Hallows at Great Mitton offers plenty of interest, with the oldest surviving section of the church originating from *c.*1270. An interesting feature is a dark oak screen separating the nave from the chancel that was brought to the church from the remote Cockersands Abbey near Cockerham in 1537 following the Dissolution. A number of tombs and exceptionally ornate memorials are to be found within the Sherburn (Shireburn) family chapel which is integrated with the church. Sir Richard Sherburn was interred there in 1594, as was his wife Maud and several descendants. In the churchyard there is a sundial dating back to 1683 and the remnants of a fourteenth-century cross. The lovely view of the Ribble and surrounding countryside from the churchyard will hopefully inspire you to continue walking towards Clitheroe along the Ribble Way.

The river Ribble and Mitton church. *Courtesy of Malcolm Greenhalgh.*

This walk makes for an altogether pleasant and exhilarating experience, especially at dawn or dusk if one wants to see bird and mammal activity. For example on the river there have been reports of otter sightings in the Clitheroe area in recent years. The otter may be making a comeback and the best time to see one is at dawn or dusk. To be in with a chance go out along the river looking for evidence of paw marks or dung, proceeding very quietly whilst keeping your eyes on the river to look for the otter's distinctive hump and motion. The river itself should produce a very good selection of typical river birds. Perseverance is usually rewarded by a glimpse of a kingfisher, often just a flash of blue as it speeds over the river. Kingfishers perch on both overhanging branches and stones so it is best to scan suitable sites, especially in the breeding season when they can be very active. Scanning the river ahead may reveal the first goosanders, easy to pick out on size alone from the regular flocks of mallard. Grey and pied wagtail and dipper favour the fast-flowing water and the latter species has been specially adapted to reach and exploit food beneath the surface of the water that other birds cannot.

At Edisford Bridge the remnants of a medieval toll bridge can be observed beneath the present bridge. The trans-Pennine crossing from the Vale of York to the Ribble estuary is traceable by a chain of Norman castles, including those at Skipton and Clitheroe. At Edisford Bridge a diversion may be taken by bus or car to visit the medieval market town of Clitheroe. The town has origins in the late twelfth century when a settlement grew up around the Norman castle, built by Roger de Lacy to protect his vast estate – 'The Honour of Clitheroe' – and to keep out the marauding Scots. The castle stands proudly on a massive outcrop of limestone and is today characterised by its post-medieval high street and the town centre that emanated from it. The keep of the castle with its impressive walls – over nine feet thick – survived the Battle of Preston of 1648, but the castle was mostly demolished by Cromwell's parliamentary forces to prevent any possibility of resurgence of this royalist stronghold. Today the keep is reputed to be the smallest Norman keep in England, though only the shell remains, together with a section of medieval wall. It is still a dominant landmark in Clitheroe and together with its gardens, laid out to commemorate the 1937 Coronation of King George VII, and museum housed in the eighteenth-century Castle House, it is well worth a visit. It is befitting that the original ferry boat that used to ply across the Ribble at Hacking Hall is now an exhibit in the museum along with other fascinating items of interest.

At Low Moor – a district of Clitheroe – the Ribble Way passes alongside allotments before reaching a combined weir and salmon leap next to Waddow Hall (run as a training centre for Girl Guides), and going on to Brungerley Bridge, which in 1814 was built to link Clitheroe with the nearby village of Waddington. After passing Brungerley Bridge the tree-lined Ribble Way passes below Brungerley Park – a recreational haven for local people particularly at the turn of the twentieth century – and onto Salthill Quarry, a former limestone quarry that was worked from at least the seventeenth century until *c*. 1910. Apart from being used by the construction industry crushed stone was burned in kilns to produce lime, and indeed the landscape of Bowland is still peppered with the industrial archaeology of the process.

Since this particular quarry was abandoned natural colonisation has occurred and areas of meadow, scrub and woodland have developed. Open areas are managed to encourage wildflowers and meadow sweet, lady's bedstraw, thyme, burnet saxifrage, crosswort, wood anemones and several species of orchid, which all thrive in the calcium-rich soil. The reserve also supports a range of bird species including jay, sparrowhawk, blackcap, garden warbler and chiffchaff, and a variety of butterflies such as red admiral, painted lady, small tortoiseshell, orange tip, speckled wood, meadow brown and the small yet distinctive common blue. An attractive sculpture trail leads through the quarry and is popular with children.

Back on the river the breeding bird of the shingle is the attractive black and white oystercatcher, whose noisy 'piping' can be heard from late January to early July. This display is all part of the territorial disputes, and an integral part of breeding-cycle behaviour. Oystercatchers also nest away from the river in the surrounding fields where lapwing and curlew struggle to find remnants of unimproved grasslands. Where the shingle is higher and more vegetated, common sandpiper may also be found. Goosanders nest high up in large holes in trees and lead their large families into the river. On hatching, the youngsters simply jump out, hopefully onto a soft landing on water. Mallards can also be seen with their broods of ducklings. Sand martins are commonly seen during spring and summer skimming the surface of the water for insects. Green woodpeckers are fairly well established in the Ribble Valley and occasionally may be seen, or more likely heard, in suitable habitats.

In the last forty years a jewel of an insect has expanded its range along rivers, canals and streams in central Lancashire and may now be seen in summer on most of the described Ribble walks. If you spot a turquoise-coloured damselfly daintily flying or perching in vegetation it is more than likely to be the banded demoiselle. The Latin name of the species is *Calopteryx Splendens*, quite appropriate for splendid they unquestionably are.

Hurst Green Circular

In the Footsteps of Tolkien along the Ribble Way

Start/finish	Start and finish at Hurst Green
Grid Ref	SD 685379
Distance	6.2 miles (10 kilometres)
Time	4 hours
Grade	Easy
General	Parking, toilet and refreshment facilities at Hurst Green

This circular walk begins and ends at Hurst Green close to Stonyhurst College at the southern boundary of the Forest of Bowland. The fabulous panorama of the college nestling in the heart of the Ribble Valley in splendid isolation, complete with its long driveway and twin lakes, towers and green copper cupolas, is certainly impressive and comes as a complete surprise to many visitors to the area. Stonyhurst was originally the home of the Shireburns, lords of the manor since medieval times until the last male heir Richard Francis Shireburn died in 1717. The oldest part of the building was begun by Hugh Shireburn in 1523 and extended by Richard Shireburn in 1592. In 1794 Stonyhurst was donated by the Weld family to the Jesuit college at Liège in France as a boarding school for Catholic boys. It was subsequently enlarged in 1799, assuming its present grandeur and alluring appearance during the early nineteenth century.

Stonyhurst College has a distinguished list of ex-pupils including Sir Arthur Conan Doyle, who evidently gained literary inspiration in his surroundings whilst attending the college between 1869 and 1875. A fellow pupil just happened to be named Patrick Sherlock, while two of Sir Arthur's contemporaries had the name of Moriarty. The author probably caught up with them in 'the dark walk' – mentioned in the *Hound of the Baskervilles* – and an eerie dark avenue with a canopy of ancient, gnarled yew trees.

Opposite The sentinel of the marsh – a grey heron. *Courtesy of Peter Smith.*

Stonyhurst College. *Courtesy of Malcolm Greenhalgh.*

This unique feature is not the only possible connection to the classic book, for the description of Baskerville Hall itself suggests that it was the ornate Stonyhurst building and its setting that provided the inspiration: 'The Avenue opened into a broad expanse of turf, and the house lay before us. In the centre was a heavy building from which a porch projected ... from the centre block raised the twin towers, ancient, crenelated and pierced with many loopholes.' The dark walk in the Jesuit Garden is similar to where Sir Charles Baskerville met his gruesome end, and to this day is as spooky as ever with doubtless the same ancient yew trees, laden with copious poisonous bright-red berries, providing a perfect hideaway for the ever-present chaffinch and nuthatch, not to mention pupils!

Stonyhurst also has links with J. R. R. Tolkien, author of *Lord of the Rings*, who was renowned for his love of nature and the natural landscape. Tolkien spent much of his time writing at Stonyhurst College while visiting his two sons who were pupils; indeed the Oxford professor is believed to have transposed the local landscape into his stories, with part of the area reputed to be the inspiration for Middle Earth. Peter Jackson, the producer of the enormously successful film trilogy, used New Zealand as the location of the fantasy land, and there are many similarities with the Bowland landscape. The idyllic location of the truly iconic architecture of the college is complemented by unspoilt countryside just below the gentle undulations of Longridge Fell. The ethereal and magical places we read about in Tolkien's writings may even be imagined here, in what seems to be a perfect haunt for hobbits. The view from Tom Bombadil's house could have been based on that from New Lodge, where Tolkien stayed. Familiar names that occur in

148

the film include Shire Lane in Hurst Green and the river Shirebourne, named after Sir Richard Shireburn. During the 1950s a small ferry service (rowing boat) known as the Hacking Ferry still operated across the river Ribble near to Hacking Hall, and was perhaps the inspiration for the Buckleberry Ferry in the *Fellowship of the Ring*. The photogenic three-arched Cromwell's Bridge, built by Sir Richard Shireburn in 1561, might have inspired Tolkien to create Brandywine Bridge on the river Brandywine. We will never really know for sure but his walks along the Hodder and Ribble, set amidst pastoral countryside against the backcloth of Pendle Hill, are believed to have influenced his writing. The Tolkien Trail follows a circular route along the rivers Hodder and Ribble, on which the river Shirebourne could well have been based. Tolkien would probably have been familiar with many of the local birds, including the sight and sound of the grey wagtail. This species and bird song are the themes of the walk that integrate a good diversity of birds to be seen in their natural habitat – or should that be 'hobitat'!

From Warren Fold in Hurst Green, cross over a stile and follow the wall. After a gateway with kissing gate, walk diagonally right across a field, passing a large tree. Turn right on reaching the hedge and go through two more kissing gates. Cross the stream and climb uphill, passing Fox Hall Wood on the left. Proceed to the gate in the right-hand corner of the field and turn right along a tarmac track to reach Hall Barn Farm. At this point there is an option to have a close view of Stonyhurst College by walking left along this public right of way to the front of the building and then retracing your

This sand martin has its work cut out feeding five chicks who are waiting eagerly for mum at the entrance to their nesthole. *Courtesy of Peter Smith.*

steps towards Hall Barn Farm to continue the walk. Turn left immediately be-
fore the farm buildings and walk straight ahead to reach Woodfields, passing
St Mary's College on the left. Cross over the road and turn down the lane be-
tween the houses. When the track bears left, turn right and go over a wooden
style, then follow the edge of the field alongside Over Hacking Wood. Near the
corner, turn left over a stile, then right to descend a stepped path.

Early spring is a good time to do this walk. The first section traverses the environs of Hurst Green and Stonyhurst, a semi-rural habitat, usually enhanced by bird song. At Hurst Green listen for the chirpings of house sparrows, for nowadays sightings of this officially endangered species are worth recording. The copses and hedgerows hold mistle thrush, song thrush, blackbird, chaffinch, titmice, greenfinch and robin, though lead vocalists do not need a podium here. A blackbird singing is something really special and its flute-like notes are in total contrast to the song thrush. Robert Browning said that 'the song of the wise thrush, he sings everything twice over'; in fact each syllable is repeated at least two or three times! Listen carefully for the murmurings of starlings, for the bird is an excellent mimic. It is a familiar though declining garden bird with a reputation for being noisy, quarrelsome and garrulous, but who could not admire its glossy and iridescent summer plumage complete with a bright-yellow bill, so why not learn to love them? Chaffinches start to 'warm up' in February with a hesitant rattle, before delivering the full trill with a terminal flourish, and dunnocks sing their wheezy little ditty of a song. Flocks of jackdaw are predominant in the fields and around Stonyhurst's majestic buildings, where in spring and summer diminishing populations of house martin and swift may be seen flying over the village's almhouses and perhaps nesting on this and other suitable buildings that comprise the college complex. The swift is built for flight and its aerodynamic build renders it capable of flying at an exceptional 60 miles per hour, commendably within the national speed limit. Furthermore they are the only birds known to mate on the wing.

During spring, Fox Hall Wood is clothed in a blaze of colour, ranging from the emerging fresh green foliage of sycamore to stunning copper beeches and glorious white cherry blossom. The pond provides an attractive feature, further enhanced by a range of common birds. The nuthatch has significantly increased over the last two decades and its vocal prowess usually belies its sedentary habits. Both great and blue tits have an extensive range of song, which pierces the early spring. Great spotted woodpeckers drum and are frequently recognised from their bouncing flight between woodland and garden. Unlike many other species, both male and female robins establish winter territories and defend them by song from late summer onwards. During cold spells most of any small birds' waking hours are taken up with feeding.

Cross over the footbridge before turning right over a stone bridge and climbing the bank towards Hodder Place. Descend to the river and follow a track along the riverbank to the main road at Lower Hodder Bridge. Turn right along the main road to reach a footpath on the left, opposite the first road junction on the right. From here the route is fairly straightforward. Cross over the stile almost opposite the bus shelter and follow the waymarkers and Ribble Way logo across fields to reach a track leading to Winkley Hall Farm and beyond, passing by a lovely English oak tree with a tremendous girth, to the banks of the Hodder at its unceremonious confluence with the Ribble. The footpath follows the Ribble for about two kilometres, eventually passing an aqueduct. After the aqueduct strike off right through a wood and ascend the valley sides to complete the walk at Hurst Green. Alternatively follow a concessionary path that skirts the top of the wood to rejoin Ribble Way at Trough House Farm. Turn right on Lambing Clough Lane to return to the starting point at Hurst Green.

Cromwell's Bridge crosses over the river Hodder near Hurst Green.
Courtesy of Malcolm Greenhalgh.

Heron, dipper and grey and pied wagtails frequent the fast-flowing river throughout the year. Listen and look for the turquoise-blue flash of a kingfisher's back as it flies close to the surface of the river. Common sandpipers can be seen in their characteristic posture on stones in the river and making brief stiff-winged flights, calling as they go. It is a sobering thought that grey wagtails and Daubenton's bats have lived alongside the picturesque packhorse bridge at Lower Hodder since it was first built by Sir Richard Shireburn in 1561. The open-sided bridge lost its parapets after the road bridge was built alongside in 1826 and is therefore potentially dangerous to cross over. However, its skeletal configurations are very attractive and it is worthy of being photographed, while taking an opportunity to observe riverine birds and to contemplate for a moment whether Cromwell crossed the bridge while en route to battle in 1648. The reality is that a bridge seven feet wide would probably have been a little narrow for an army of 10,000 infantry and cavalry. Cromwell and his officers probably enjoyed the luxury of not getting their feet wet, while the rain-soaked army probably had to ford the river. Some historians would consign this fanciful legend to the romantic story bin, for current debate is that the crossing was actually upstream at Higher Hodder. However, what is not disputed is that Oliver Cromwell made the decision to advance westwards along the north bank of the Ribble to cut off the Scots, and spent the pre-battle night sleeping on a table whilst in full armour at Stonyhurst. Cromwell said of the building that it was 'the finest Elizabethan half house I have ever seen'.

On the approach to Winckley Hall Farm around 15 pairs of heron build huge nests and rear strange-looking youngsters in the tree-top heronry. The bizarre goings on at the heronry deserve observation, if only to see the adults flying in, uttering a loud 'krowrnk' and swaying on delicate-looking branches. Who knows, it may even have inspired Tolkein to write about hobbits, for a young heron has an equally peculiar form and perhaps bears the closest resemblance!

Continuing along the Ribble Way, watch for a little owl in the mature trees and hedgerows that bisect fields, where a few pairs of lapwing attempt to nest in fields of maize and other suitable places. Kestrels hover over open spaces and sparrowhawks characteristically patrol hedgerows, relying on an element of surprise in catching their exclusively avian prey. Blackcap, garden warbler, willow warbler and chiffchaff are typical spring migrants that haunt the wooded areas close to the Hodder and Ribble.

Opposite Painting of a kingfisher perched by the river Hodder, featuring Cromwell's three-arched bridge of 1561. *Watercolour by Norman Duerden, FRSA.*

The river Hodder takes a meandering course through wooded valleys.
Courtesy of Malcolm Greenhalgh.

At the confluence of the Calder and the Ribble one can reflect on the history of the location by observing the isolation of the former rebuilt ferry house on the north bank and Hacking Hall on the south bank, a large Jacobean house with many mullioned windows that was built on the site of a medieval manor house. On the north bank are two mounds, thought to be burial places of Saxon warriors engaged in battle during AD 798. Relics of the battle have been unearthed, including a stone coffin found in 1836 containing human bones and implements of war. Close to where the rowing boat went to and fro across the river, serving locals and hikers until closure in the 1950s, I have observed tree sparrows on several occasions. During spring and summer sand martins fly over the river from colonies in the riverbanks. Depending on the time of year, highlights of birdwatching along the Ribble Way past the confluence and the graceful lines of the white aqueduct may include greenshank and green sandpiper, as well as kingfisher, dipper, grey wagtail, oystercatcher, curlew, whimbrel, common sandpiper, redshank and goldeneye. Goosander may also be seen throughout the year and during springtime are often accompanied by a brood of ducklings swimming along with the adult female. Finally, after leaving the river choose between the two aforementioned options to return to Hurst Green and the starting point of the walk.

Hurst Green Circular via Bayley Hall

Start/finish	Start and finish at the war memorial at Hurst Green
Grid Ref	685379
Distance	3.7 miles (6 kilometres)
Time	3 hours
Grade	Easy
General	Refreshment and toilet facilities at Hurst Green. This is another attractive walk commencing from Hurst Green and featuring birds of open country and woodland

This circular treasure trail embraces the Ribble Valley, with pleasant scenery, wildlife and sites of historic interest, but is slightly different in that no further clues are given. The challenge is to discover sites of historic interest for yourself and to identify and record your own list of birds. A careful approach within the environs of Hurst Green should reveal one or two surprises. Happy hunting!

Commencing from the war memorial at Hurst Green walk along the main road (B6243) to the church of St John the Evangelist and there follow a waymarked track (left) to Merrick Hall Farm. Continue across a field and into Bayley Hall Wood where the path crosses over a footbridge and emerges at the ancient Bayley Hall Farm. Continue along the farm track to the B6243, turn left along the main road for a short distance, then first right and proceed along a bridleway. Approaching the second of two farms at the end of the track follow the path left across a field and enter Hud Lee Wood – a mixed coniferous and deciduous wood – before emerging onto a bridleway. Turn right along the bridleway and after passing the interesting Greengore dwelling (right) fork left at a Y-junction to descend to the bridge over Dean Brook. Follow the obvious path back through the wood, past the cottages and onto the tarmac road and then right to the starting point of the walk.

Opposite The little owl haunts hedgerows, copses and farm buildings around Preston and is a likely candidate to be observed on most of the described walks. *Courtesy of Peter Smith.*

Ribchester to Hurst Green

via Suspension Bridge

Start/finish   Start at Ribchester; finish at Hurst Green
Grid Ref   649353
Distance   4 miles (6.5 kilometres)
Time   4 hours
Grade   Easy
General   Parking, toilet and refreshment facilities at Ribchester
                 and Hurst Green. Ribchester Museum is open weekdays
                 between 09:00–17:00 and 12:00–17:00 at weekends

This is another attractive history-themed walk featuring birds of open country and woodland. Please refer to the previous river Ribble Tolkien bird-watching walk described above for an indication of some of the typical species likely to be encountered along a similar section of the Ribble.

From the centre of Ribchester walk along the main road towards Blackburn and cross over the Ribble bridge; immediately thereafter turn left and proceed along the road towards Dinkley, passing Salesbury Hall (left) to reach Marles Wood where the road ascends a steep hill. Nearing the top of the hill branch off left along a footpath and cross over a footbridge to take a well-defined footpath along the banks of the Ribble, eventually arriving at the attractive Dinkley suspension bridge. Cross over the bridge to reach Trough House Farm and walk the full length of a minor road quaintly known as Lambing Clough Lane, to reach Hurst Green. Alternatively complete a circular walk back to Ribchester by following the Ribble Way logos along the north bank of the river Ribble commencing at Trough House.

Opposite   The Roman road from Ribchester to Preston and the Fylde (Watling Street) is here discernable at Elston, Grimsargh. *Author's collection.*

The Roman bath house, Ribchester. *Courtesy of Malcolm Greenhalgh.*

We begin this walk at the village of Ribchester, prettily situated on the banks of the Ribble and steeped in Roman history. Even the White Bull pub is graced with what are believed to be Roman pillars at the entrance porch. To the rear of the pub are the foundations of a Roman bath house comprising cold baths, hot baths and even the luxury of a hypocaust (underfloor heating system). Close by is the thirteenth-century church of St Wilfrid and alongside it the Museum of Roman Antiquities which flanks fort earthworks – and all occupying a delightful riverside site.

Following the Roman invasion of southern England in AD 43, advancing Roman legions intent on conquering northern England had a challenging time defeating the region's Celtic tribes. The Celts were well established in the North West and Roman onslaughts involved armies landing by sea and using the Ribble and Lune valleys for inland penetration. Overland advances involved the construction of roads linking the forts at Chester, Manchester, Ribchester, Lancaster and Kirkham. Just after this conquest, a military supplies depot was set up at Walton-le-Dale. Situated alongside the Ribble and astride the road running north, and by an established ford crossing, it was strategically important and within reach of the fort at Ribchester. *Bremetennacum Veteranorum*, the Roman name for Ribchester, was at the heart of the road network. The fort was probably built between AD 75 and 80 by Agricola during his campaign against the Brigantes and provided for the accommodation of a cavalry troop of at least 500 men.

Despite the initial conflict, day-to-day life involved the people working on the land to sustain the rural economy and experiencing a peaceful co-existence for the greater part of the occupation, which lasted for over 300 years. Settlement patterns and ways of life do not appear to have been greatly affected by the Roman occupation, nor by their departure. This was in contrast to the southern counties where the effects of Romanisation were much greater. The roads enabled soldiers and supplies to be moved quickly between trouble spots. Tracing the course of the road at Ribchester may be accomplished with a trained eye and the help of the staff at the Ribchester Roman Museum, which is well worth a visit to see the collection of Roman artefacts. Just beyond Ribchester's museum, St Wilfrid's offers much historical interest, including a seveneenth-century sundial with the intriguing inscription, *I am a shadow, so art thou. I mark time, dost thou?* The present church occupies the site of an earlier church which probably dated back to the seventh century and St Wilfrid, to whom the current church is dedicated. Ribchester was probably at the centre of the estates on the Ribble which were granted to Wilfrid's Abbey at Ripon in AD 670. The interior of the church is normally accessible.

Having absorbed some of the history at the church and museum enjoy the lovely view across the river. During springtime watch the busy

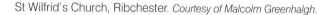

St Wilfrid's Church, Ribchester. *Courtesy of Malcolm Greenhalgh.*

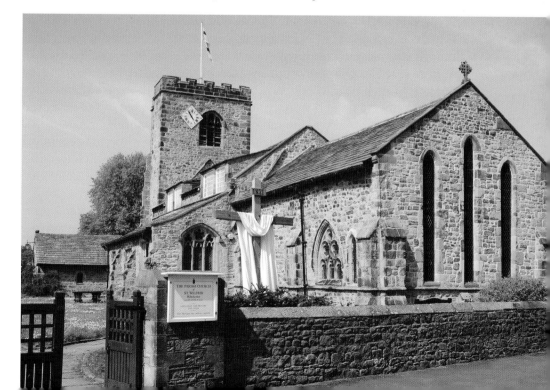

sand martin colony on the opposite bank, perhaps a heron or two fishing furtively, and farmyard geese or any other birds that may give themselves up! In moments of quiet contemplation reflect on the schoolboy who in the eighteenth century found a magnificent bronze Roman ceremonial helmet which now features as an important exhibit in the British Museum, though a replica is in the Ribchester Roman Museum. Leaving Ribchester why not seek out two very interesting buildings at Stydd by taking a minor diversion by the Ribchester hotel. The first of these is the distinctive façade of the almshouse which was built c. 1726. The striking two-storey building comprises a balustrade veranda formed by four Tuscan columns, giving the building a unique character. Close by is all that is left of the oldest church building in the valley, the tiny twelfth-century Stydd church.

Returning to the main road, after a mile or so we cross over the three graceful arches of a strategic bridge built in 1776. The river Ribble and the sharp contours of its valley have helped to preserve the relatively unspoilt countryside between Preston and the upper reaches, and industrialisation has, to this day, not impacted too heavily upon the landscape. There are still no road bridges between the Preston city boundary at Brockholes and this bridge at Ribchester, for there was little incentive to build important roads alongside the north bank of the meandering river.

Turn left along the road towards Dinkley to reach the point where the river passes 'Sale Wheel' and adjacent woodlands on either side. At Marles Wood we cross over a wooden footbridge spanning a small wooded ravine – perfect habitat for the wren. This ubiquitous bird is likely to be located moving through the complex maze of ground cover and along the bank.

Hereabouts the exceedingly illusive and rare lesser spotted woodpecker has in the past made a few guest appearances for unsuspecting birdwatchers, although not recently. Nationally since the 1970s we have lost four out of five pairs of lesser spots and in many parts of the UK they have disappeared completely. Leaving the woods behind, the walk follows the banks of the Ribble until suddenly the natural world is interrupted by the sight of the delightful Dinkley suspension bridge looming into view. The footbridge replaced the Dinkley Ferry in 1951. Why not linger on the bridge for a while, for, depending on the season, it affords a good vantage point from which to watch the river complete with its small parties of goosander, goldeneye, common sandpiper, pied and grey wagtail and perhaps even a kingfisher if you're lucky!

We now enter the final section of the walk where the path joins Lambing Clough Lane and gradually ascends to Hurst Green. On private land near Lambing Clough Lane, where garden warblers sing so beautifully in springtime, there is an interesting abandoned railway cutting, isolated in

Dinkley suspension bridge replaced a ferry crossing in 1951 and is a pleasing feature of this walk. *Courtesy of Malcolm Greenhalgh.*

the middle of a field. This was to be the course of the Fleetwood, Preston and West Riding Junction Railway which was never built and now graces the landscape as a folly and a monument to an ill-fated Victorian enterprise. When I obtained permission to visit the site, I enjoyed an interesting encounter with this little-known, but nonetheless significant, railway landmark. Whilst standing in the cutting, I took time to reflect upon its legacy, for there is something poignant about this place, which brings to mind the challenges, expectations and aspirations of the early Victorian railway speculators at the height of railway mania.

The abandoned project to extend the railway through the Ribble Valley was described by Dobson in 1877: 'We saw for some distance an excavation, with level bottom and sloping sides, continuing to the next dingle there was again the beginning of an embankment, as if to cross over the valley through which runs Clough Brook. I soon saw that this was a detached and uncompleted portion of that once ambitious project, the Fleetwood, Preston, and West Riding Junction railway. The Act for making this railway was passed in the year 1846. It was to utilise the Preston and Longridge line by branching off that line below Grimsargh, and pass via Hothersall, Dutton, Hurst Green, and Mitton to Whalley and into Yorkshire.' Nestling in splendid isolation the cutting is clearly recognisable as a detached section of that once ambitious project.

'Whistling Down the Wind'

Beautiful Downham
& Twiston Beck

Start/finish	Start and finish at Downham – car park in centre of village
Grid Ref	785442
Distance	4.3 miles (7 kilometres)
Time	3–4 hours
Grade	Easy
General	Refreshment and toilet facilities at Downham

From the main car park in Downham walk to the bridge over Downham Beck and follow the path left alongside the beck, later indicated by waymarkers. Cross over stiles and a footbridge before ascending higher ground to an isolated barn. Turn left here and cross a gully. At a junction of paths fork left across a field towards the indicated Hecklin Farm. Approaching Hecklin Farm cross over a stile (left) at the end of the wall and follow a descending route across a field, indicated by small boulders.

At the bottom of the hill turn right and cross a stile alongside a gate. Follow the waymarked path alongside a fence, eventually passing over a stile leading into an overgrown lane which emerges into a field. Turn right and follow the edge of the field downhill turning right at Twiston Brook and then cross over the footbridge. Go left past Twiston Mill pond before turning right onto a minor road. After a short distance pass through a kissing gate on the left. Follow the path alongside the beck, eventually reaching a footbridge; cross the bridge and walk uphill to reach Springs Farm.

Opposite top   The abandoned railway cutting at Hurst Green today plays host to flocks of sheep. Author's collection.

Opposite bottom   The picturesque village of Downham in front of Pendle Hill. Courtesy of Graham Wilkinson.

Beyond the farm cross over two stiles whilst heading for a prominent group of trees on higher ground and then cross a wall stile. Veer slightly right across a field and then straight on past a long-disused small quarry on the left next to a stile. Pass over another stile and then a kissing gate next to a concessionary path. Turn right towards Hey House Farm and at the farm turn left over a stone stile, then follow the path towards a wood. After the wood take the wide field ridge which is the route of a Roman road and head towards another wood before turning left to reach the Assheton Arms at Downham and the starting point of the walk.

The beautiful village of Downham has seen very little change over the past two centuries, so where better to start than by exploring the village that is renowned for being one of the prettiest in Lancashire. Its charm lies in its idyllic location dominated by the isolated and ever-watchful Pendle Hill, and the village's picturesque cottages, medieval church and stone bridge over Twiston Beck. Downham is an estate village where the Assheton family have been lords of the manor of Downham Hall since 1558. The buildings are of a similar age and then, as now, conform to particular architectural styles, and there are strict rules about modern additions. This means that the village is devoid of satellite dishes and aerials and not marred by ugly yellow lines or anything that would spoil its overall appearance.

Not surprisingly Downham has provided an ideal set for many films. These include *Whistle down the Wind* (1961) starring Hayley Mills and Alan Bates, which featured the village, though it was mostly shot nearby at Worsow End Farm, with local young actors excelling in the superb roles and gangs of local schoolchildren being drafted in for the crowd scenes. This classic film epitomised rural life enhanced by the local landscapes, and further enriched by the songs and calls of local birds, which included the curlew and the ever-present flocks of jackdaw. Birds define an environment, both in their song and in their visual presence, and that environment devoid of its principal acts of the natural world is like a film without its leading actors. Although the local jackdaw flocks remain it is unlikely that you will these days encounter the specialities of Bowland such as ring ousel or hen harrier on this route, though when birding anything is possible!

Begin by checking the garden bird feeders for visiting finches, nuthatch, blue tit, great tit and coal tit and other visiting birds throughout the year. During spring concentrate on listening to the liquid gold notes of the

Opposite   Barn owl on a lichen- and snow-covered post. *Courtesy of Peter Smith.*

blackbird or the repetitious, intriguing call of the song thrush, surely a sound that will lift any spirit. Both pied and grey wagtail haunt the stream in the village, close to the bridge where there is always a flock of tame well-fed mallard. The great spotted woodpecker has adapted to gardens nowadays but more typically may be found in copses and hedgerows along the walk; the latter also being the haunt of flocks of Scandinavian thrush during winter. This is a walk to be enjoyed throughout the seasons, especially on a nice spring day; interesting birds likely to feature include curlew, lapwing, pied and grey wagtail, willow warbler and redstart, which may be seen in a landscape largely shaped by the activities of man during the Middle Ages.

Farming during this period involved a system of common open fields rotated for arable use and probably provided for at least one cultivated field, being close to the settlement. Common pasturage was gradually replaced by the divisions of farming land into more consolidated holdings. Enclosure schemes gradually superseded the medieval structure of open fields as the land owned by the lord of the manor was leased to tenants and the medieval strips disappeared under the grass.

Forming a backcloth to a predominance of farmland countryside and the wooded valley of Twiston Beck is a fantastic vista of Pendle Hill and the Bowland and Yorkshire fells dominated by Penyghent which is to be enjoyed throughout the walk. The north face of Pendle Hill slopes steeply down to the Ribble Valley. The hill itself is composed of coarse-grained millstone grit sandstone and this enduring rock, along with carboniferous limestone elements, forms the Pennines. Limestone is used for making cement and the large twin chimneys at Clitheroe rather sully the picturesque landscape and reveal the site of a cement factory.

Twiston Beck offers a contrasting habitat for birds and other wildlife, especially if one is lucky enough to observe a redstart. During spring this very attractive summer visitor often sings from the tallest trees alongside the beck, which is also a favoured habitat of spotted flycatchers. Pause on the footbridges crossing the beck to check for dipper, grey wagtail and common sandpiper. Little owls are occasionally seen in daylight in the vicinity of Springs Farm, typically perched on the fence posts, walls or in trees, so look out for their undulating flight. Both redstart and pied wagtail use holes in the stone walls for nesting sites. Stock doves may be seen flying over pasture and swallows still nest in most of the farm outbuildings along with a few house sparrows.

Returning to Downham, take time to reflect on the lovely scenery. The surrounding countryside hosts breeding kestrel, buzzard, sparrowhawk, tawny owl, little owl and barn owl. Around the village and agricultural land, that Asiatic invader of the late 1960s, the collared dove, is a familiar species, having extended its range across Europe from the early 1930s. The first British sighting was in Lincolnshire in 1952. It first bred in Lancashire in 1961 and is now well established in the county.

During high summer Downham is complemented by the sight and sound of the swift, flying into the roof voids of pretty terraced cottages and ancient buildings. Flocks of them scream and wheel overhead in a frenzied communal display. Swifts are sadly in decline as modern and restored buildings no longer facilitate access to the roof space for swifts to build their flimsy nests of straw and feathers. However, this can be addressed with the provision of swift nesting boxes located under the eaves and/or small spaces left for them. Swifts fly hundreds of miles a day whilst feeding exclusively on airborne insects. There is one record of an individual bird attaining 16 years of age; in its lifetime it would have flown an estimated four million miles, enough to take it to the moon and back eight times – what a fabulous aeronaut *and* bird!

Perhaps a fitting way to conclude this walk would be to sit down comfortably with a pint of cask ale outside the village pub and enjoy the spectacle of a flock of swifts.

Whitewell Circular

via Radholme Laund

Start/finish	Start and finish at the Inn at Whitewell
Grid Ref	658468
Distance	4 miles (6.5 kilometres)
Time	3–4 hours
Grade	Easy
General	Toilet, refreshement and parking facilities at Whitewell

This is another interesting circular walk through diverse countryside, with the opportunity to spot several of Bowland's familiar birds in an historic landscape.

From Whitewell village hall take the road uphill past the village hall towards Clitheroe. After a short distance climb the steps on the right. Keeping right of Seed Hill Farm ascend the steep hill by going straight ahead to reach a wall stile (above a hollow). Cross over the stile and follow the path alongside the nearby right-hand wall. Pass through two kissing gates close to Higher Top Barn (left) before reaching Radholme Laund. Go through the farmyard and follow the waymarkers through fields to pass alongside a woodland on the left. Cross over a stile and veer right across a field towards a gate/stile to take a track leading to Higher Lees Farm. At Higher Lees the footpath leads straight ahead, then descends left to the brook. Follow the markers, crossing over stiles on the right-hand side of the brook, then crossing over a footbridge leading to the Clitheroe road and turn right to reach a T-junction. At the junction walk along the main road towards the wooded Whitewell Gorge. Just before reaching the gorge look for a footpath sign on the right and take the field footpath that broadly parallels the Whitewell Gorge, eventually reaching Seed Hill Farm and the starting point of the walk.

Opposite A fieldfare shows off its best side for the camera. *Courtesy of Peter Smith.*

Otter. *Courtesy of Peter Smith.*

Historically Bowland was part of the old forest of the North and the royal hunting forest of Lancaster – Bolland. The Old Norse is a derivative of 'Bu' (cattle) or the Celtic 'Booa', a cow, signifying 'cowland'. Following the Norman Conquest the Forest of Bolland (Bowland) was a deer forest; however, forest is a misnomer in that the 18,000 acres established by the de Lacy family was never extensively wooded. It was Gisburn Forest that saw blanket afforestation and was the largest in Lancashire as a twentieth-century development. The forecourt of the Inn at Whitewell was once the location of the local market for the district. The hotel was built on the site occupied by the former fourteenth-century hunting lodge where the keeper of the royal forest of Bowland, Walter Urswyck, resided. Walter established a chapel at Whitewell next to the inn at the beginning of the fifteenth century, although the present chapel only dates back to 1818.

The name 'Radholme' has Norse origins and refers only to a settlement on the flat upland plain between Whitewell and Cow Ark, where today the transformed landscape affords stunning views of the Hodder Valley throughout this walk. Officers of the chase of Bolland had responsibility for the red and fallow deer within the curtilage of Radholme deer park. Special areas called launds were set aside before they were released into the designated hunting areas. Radholme was one of two deer parks within the forest; the other was situated at Leagram. During the thirteenth century the gradual conversion of substantial parts of the Forest of Bowland to vaccaries (dairy farms) and pasture led to its eventual demise as a hunting ground, and although archaeological evidence of the deer park may still be discerned, today it is essentially dairy pasture. Nowadays, roe deer and the introduced sika deer have replaced the red and fallow deer herds of Radholme Laund. Whilst walking over the limestone hills to the farm at Radholme Laund

Pheasant – there is no shortage of this species throughout Bowland.
Courtesy of Peter Smith.

we can reflect that the land it is built on was once occupied by a thatched timber lodge where the custodians of the deer park were based.

Soaring buzzards are a prominent feature over the Whitewell Gorge and they may be seen in aerial disputes with carrion crows over the wooded ravine and grasslands. In spring the fields around Whitewell still have lapwing and curlew that have probably greeted travellers since pre-history, though for how much longer? The varied habitat of today also supports snipe, moorhen, mallard, nuthatch and reed bunting. During summer, swallow, swift, redstart, willow warbler, chiffchaff, blackcap and garden warbler return from Africa to their prime habitats in and around the village and gorge. Large flocks of wintering birds of Scandinavian origin, including

Flocks of jay may be found in the Whitewell Gorge. *Courtesy of Peter Smith.*

redwing and fieldfare, may be seen anywhere on this walk. Bramblings have a preference for beech mast and are occasionally seen with chaffinch flocks in the Whitewell Gorge or close to the Inn at Whitewell. Chaffinches start to 'warm up' in February with a hesitant rattle, before delivering their full and welcome song. The origin of the name chaffinch harks back to a time when birds were generally much commoner than they are today – a time long before agricultural mechanisation. In those halcyon days early farming practice saw large flocks of chaffinch feeding in the corn fields, literally sorting out 'the wheat from the chaff' by feeding on the seeds or grain husks of the chaff. Almost inevitably, groups of pheasant strut about peacefully, at least until the next shoot, and sparrowhawks hunt along the hedgerows and woodland fringe. Green and great spotted woodpeckers, tawny owl, jay, nuthatch, treecreeper, goldcrest and siskin are all possibilities along woodland fringes and gardens. The unpredictability of birding is always enjoyable and there should be plenty of opportunities to record different species during this walk.

Browsholme Hall: the jewel in the crown
Browsholme via Crimptons to Whitewell

Start/finish	Start at Browsholme Hall; finish at Whitewell
Grid Ref	685454
Distance	4 miles (6.5 kilometres)
Time	4–6 hours depending on any time spent at Browsholme Hall
Grade	Easy
General	Parking, toilet and refreshment facilities at Whitewell
	A bus service links Clitheroe with Bowland and runs via Browsholme Hall

The Tudor Browsholme Hall has, since 1507, been the family seat of the Parker family. Their ancestors were the original park keepers of Radholme deer park in the Middle Ages and hereditary bowbearers (deputy administrator) of the Forest of Bolland (Bowland). Browsholme Hall is crammed with interesting artefacts collected by successive generations of the family and to find out more about its fascinating history a visit on an official open day is highly recommended.

Turn off the main road at the lodge – the main entrance to Browsholme Hall – and immediately take the track on the left that climbs above the estate. Cross the cattle grid and climb up the field to the right of a wood. Walk through two gates and, following waymarkers, veer right to cross a field and a wooden gate beside a pond. Keep left of the pond before crossing diagonally left across a field, heading towards the landmark spire at Spire Farm. Cross over a stile and follow the left-hand fence over a stone stile onto a farm track leading onto a tarmac road. Turn right onto the road, descending a steep hill to take the first

Opposite The wise old (tawny) owl is rarely encountered during daylight hours.
Courtesy of Peter Smith.

left along a track to Crimpton. Turn right on the short diversionary route and regain the footpath. Keep left to the corner of the pine wood and follow the track through the pines to emerge on the hillside with more splendid views. Walk down the hill to the right of the plantation and cross over stiles to reach the road to Whitewell. Pass through the gate on the other side of the road by the old lime kiln, continuing in the direction of Seed Hill Farm. Descending along the path through the gateway and onto the road, turn left to reach Whitewell.

In peripheral areas of the Browsholme estate, crossbills can sometimes be located during winter. Also in winter expect to see large flocks of redwing and fieldfare and mixed finch flocks of chaffinch and brambling. Sparrowhawks hunt along the hedges and open areas of the estate, where the hall is set in a landscaped park in the style of Capability Brown. Spotted and pied flycatchers, great spotted woodpecker, redstart, jay, raven, wood pigeon, reed bunting, and nuthatch are all likely suspects and the melodic tones of the blackbird, song thrush and mistle thrush enhance the overall atmosphere. Ravens may be spotted flying in tandem and engaging in a spectacular display. If there are any 'leftovers', rabbit or otherwise, they will find the tasty morsels! Nowadays there could well be a buzzard with an ever-present reception committee of carrion crows mobbing the raptor.

The ubiquitous pied wagtail is often to be found around buildings and old stone walls. *Courtesy of Peter Smith.*

The picturesque Hodder Valley is there to be enjoyed throughout the year. *Author's collection.*

On the higher ground, cuckoo, snipe, curlew, meadow pipit, sparrowhawk, peregrine, barn owl, tawny owl, short-eared owl and kestrel may be seen over these lonely Bowland moors near to Crimpton Farm. Leaving the conifer plantation, where goldcrest, siskin, chaffinch and coal tit all typically occur, you gain good views of the Hodder Valley.

Take a short break to enjoy the superb view and reflect on what lies before you: the green serenity of the Hodder Valley and its backcloth of green hillocks overshadowed by Parlick, Saddle Fell, Burnslack, Fair Oak Fell and Totridge. One can imagine that time has stood still since the Middle Ages, though at the beginning of the nineteenth century a new road penetrated the gorge and passed by the village inn situated on the beautiful banks of the Hodder. Instead of cars and tourists there would have been men driving laden packhorses and perhaps a local farmer crossing over the stepping stones of the Hodder before returning to New Laund after going about his business at the local market. New Laund was originally a keeper's house of the great forest, and then, as now, deer frequented the fields of Radholme and brown hare, fox and badger were probably abundant. We can still delight in the glorious sounds of skylarks ascending and dropping like a stone, and drumming snipe, merrily

PROPOSED LONGRIDGE & HELLIFIELD LIGHT RAILWAY OF NOVᴿ 1917.

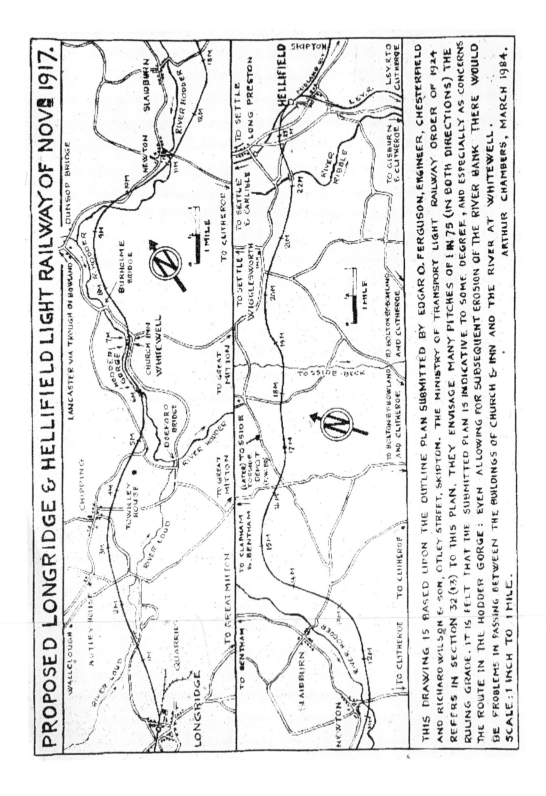

THIS DRAWING IS BASED UPON THE OUTLINE PLAN SUBMITTED BY EDGAR O. FERGUSON, ENGINEER, CHESTERFIELD AND RICHARD WILSON & SON, OTLEY STREET, SKIPTON. THE MINISTRY OF TRANSPORT LIGHT RAILWAY ORDER OF 1924 REFERS IN SECTION 32(b3) TO THIS PLAN. THEY ENVISAGE MANY PITCHES OF 1 IN 75 (IN BOTH DIRECTIONS) THE RULING GRADE. IT IS FELT THAT THE SUBMITTED PLAN IS INDICATIVE TO SOME DEGREE, AND ESPECIALLY AS CONCERNS THE ROUTE IN THE HODDER GORGE: EVEN ALLOWING FOR SUBSEQUENT EROSION OF THE RIVER BANK THERE WOULD BE PROBLEMS IN PASSING BETWEEN THE BUILDINGS OF CHURCH & INN AND THE RIVER AT WHITEWELL.

ARTHUR CHAMBERS, MARCH 1984.

SCALE: 1 INCH TO 1 MILE.

displaying over rush fields; the landscape surely has all the ingredients of a Turner or Constable masterpiece.

During the early twentieth century, however, the view would have been radically altered had plans for yet another railway line gone ahead. In 1917 railway engineer Edgar Ferguson surveyed a 24-mile route for a single-track railway running from Longridge to link with the Midland Railway at Hellifield. The branch was intended to have stations at Chipping, Whitewell, Dunsop Bridge, Newton, Slaidburn, Tosside and Wigglesworth. At Whitewell the proposed route would have passed through the gorge, alongside the river Hodder and between the church and the inn. It transpired following protracted negotiations concerning a number of complex issues that the plans for the extended railway were finally abandoned in May 1924.

Descending from the viewpoint at Raven Scar plantation, the landscape of southern Bowland is still characterised by a different industrial legacy, in the form of old lime kilns and mineral workings. Furthermore, a welcoming hostelry now awaits you, a perfect venue for further indulgence in local history, not to mention gastronomic delights and perhaps even a pint.

Opposite Imagine this railway running through the Whitewell Gorge and the heart of Bowland! *Courtesy of Malcolm Greenhalgh.*

Dunsop Bridge

via Burholme Circular

Start/finish	Start and finish at Dunsop Bridge
Grid Ref	SD 661501
Distance	4 miles (6.5 kilometres)
Time	4 hours
Grade	Easy to moderate
General	Parking, toilet and refreshment facilities at Dunsop Bridge

A feature of the walk is the Gothic Knowlmere Manor, built in the late Victorian era and once the home of the Peel family, descendants of Sir Robert Peel, the founder of the police force. The walk begins and ends at Dunsop Bridge, which in 1992 was declared by the Ordnance Survey to be the village nearest to the exact centre of the British Isles, the precise location being above the Brennand Valley. The birds likely to be seen reflect the diversity of habitat, including scenic stretches of the Hodder Valley. We pass close to Burholme, the site of a hamlet of medieval origin, and on over isolated moorland and the valley of the Hodder, usually without seeing a soul. This is perhaps one of the joys of Bowland, for even at the height of the season, few places nowadays offer such solitude.

From Dunsop Bridge car park, walk east along the road to Thorneyholme by forking right at the first junction. Cross the bridge and at the end of the railings turn right through the gate and walk the footpath following the river Hodder, to the single seventeenth-century farmstead at Burholme. Approaching the farm, turn left before the bridge over Fielding Clough and cross over a stile. Follow the yellow waymarkers to cross a second stile over a wire fence. Climb uphill with the fence on your left and Fielding Clough on the right. Walk onto the open moorland of Hodder Bank Fell and pass through a gate,

Opposite   The river Hodder from Burholme Bridge. *Courtesy of Graham Wilkinson.*

A drake goosander reflects in the river Hodder. *Courtesy of Peter Smith.*

keeping close to a barn on the right. After the barn, cross stiles while descending to the Hodder Valley. Go straight ahead onto a concessionary path turning to Knowlemere Manor and carry straight on following the yellow waymarkers past Mossthwaite, returning to Dunsop Bridge.

Flocks of swift, swallow and house martin, and the less attractive jackdaw, are invariably present around the village of Dunsop Bridge. Nowadays it is not unusual to see flocks of buzzard soaring over the Hodder and Dunsop valleys in this vicinity. The wooded area at Thorneyholme is impressive with its avenue of giant sequoia Wellingtonia; watch for the tiny goldcrest, treecreeper, nuthatch and coal tit, whilst the river provides opportunities to see some of the resident species including dipper, grey and pied wagtail, kingfisher, moorhen, mallard and goosander. During spring and summer, common sandpiper, redshank, curlew and oystercatcher are seen regularly. The scattered trees and copses on the hillside of Mossthwaite Fell and Fielding Clough used to hold cuckoo, and nowadays a chance sighting is still noteworthy. Redstart, treecreeper, chaffinch, green and great spotted woodpecker, on the other hand, are perhaps more likely to be seen.

It is hard to imagine that the single farmstead at Burholme was once the site of a fourteenth-century hamlet with a church, and may even have been mentioned in the Domesday Book as Bogewrde. The farmhouse of today is of seventeenth-century origin, evidenced by a barn dated 1619 and the initials T. S. (Thomas Swindlehurst). Close by, redshank, dipper, oystercatcher and sand martin are commonly seen along the stretch of the Hodder between the farm and the two arches of the landmark eighteenth-century Burholme Bridge. Around Burholme Farm look for goldfinch, starling, kestrel, common gull, lapwing, curlew, mallard and teal. In and around the alders in Fielding Clough leading onto the open moor, stonechat, meadow pipit, kestrel, buzzard, peregrine and short-eared owl are to be found. Buzzards often pass overhead giving their mewing call, while the harsh call of the raven announces its presence.

After passing Knowlemere Manor you reach the tiny hamlet of Mossthwaite where the track becomes a footpath. Continue along the path – often muddy underfoot – to a stile on the right. Cross over the stile and head diagonally right across the field to a fence/stile. Follow the yellow waymarkers along the edge of a field and riverbank to go through a gate at Thorneyholme. Turn right over the bridge, enter the drive, and return to the starting point at Dunsop Bridge.

Knowlemere Manor is impressive with its Gothic-style gables, numerous chimneys and adjoining parkland. Here the habitat is suitable for redstart, jay, great spotted woodpecker, nuthatch and mistle thrush. The mistle thrush is a real harbinger of spring, its melancholic song heard from the tops of the very highest trees heralds the new season like a breath of fresh air, though its country name 'stormcock' is said to forecast rain and stormy weather. Bird parties flitting through the trees comprise titmice, goldcrest, treecreeper and wren. Finches are represented at different times of year by chaffinch, greenfinch, goldfinch, bullfinch, linnet, siskin, and in some winters, brambling. Flowing though the estate the Hodder has goosander, dipper and pied and grey wagtail, and grey heron stand around motionless as they quietly fish the river before flying off on broad wings. As you pass the farmsteads, trees and pasture on the final section of the walk past Mossthwaite, look for pied wagtail, reed bunting, redstart, stock dove and curlew. Up to mid-April, fieldfares and redwings congregate in mixed flocks prior to their long flight north.

Whitewell Circular

via Hodder Gorge &
Dinkling Green

Start/finish	Start and finish at the Inn at Whitewell
Grid Ref	SD 658468
Distance	9.3 miles (15 kilometres)
Time	6 hours
Grade	Easy to moderate
General	Parking, toilet and refreshment facilities at Whitewell

We begin our walk at the car park of the Inn at Whitewell next to the chapel. Proceed left to the public footpath leading down to the edge of the river and walk the short distance to the stepping stones. A novelty of this walk is crossing the river Hodder by using these stones, but do bear in mind that any such stones might be submerged and slippery. If conditions are unsafe you have the option of crossing the river at Burholme Bridge to reach New Laund. After crossing the river ascend the slope to the farm of New Laund. Follow the footpath left at New Laund, continuing to follow the yellow waymarkers right, to climb onto a limestone knoll, where a superb vista unfolds of the Hodder threading its way through a wooded gorge set against the background of the long mass of Longridge Fell. To the north there are equally good views of the Hodder Valley and the foothills leading to the Trough of Bowland – a choice location for a picnic lunch.

Close to the Inn at Whitewell look out for redstart, chiffchaff, blackcap, garden warbler, willow warbler and occasional migrant wood warblers passing through the gorge. Coal tits are commonly encountered but the marsh tit, seen occasionally near the inn, is in definite decline. In winter

Opposite The Bowland Fell named Totridge. *Author's collection.*

The hidden hamlet of Dinkling Green. *Author's collection.*

expect to see big flocks of redwing and fieldfare and mixed flocks of chaffinch, greenfinch, bullfinch and brambling. Crossing over the stepping stones of the Hodder can be quite exhilarating, if a little damp. On the opposite bank look out for the resident dipper, kingfisher and pied and grey wagtails. Summer sees oystercatcher, redshank, common sandpiper, swift, swallow and sand martin. The path at New Laund Farm branches left and ascends above the steeply sided and extensively wooded Whitewell Gorge, where in spring the woodland harbours redstart and pied flycatcher, chiffchaff, treecreeper, nuthatch, great spotted and green woodpeckers and coal and long-tailed tits.

Follow the hillside path above the Hodder Valley and gradually descend to go over a wall stile. Skirt a field to reach a farm track leading to the hamlet of Fair Oak. Turn right by a shippon and cross the field diagonally heading towards the left side of a row of trees before crossing over two stiles onto the roadway. Walk right along the road to an isolated telephone box – at the time of writing still extant – situated at a crossroads and carry straight along a track leading to Dinkling Green.

Dinkling Green is a small settlement nestling in a landscape of verdant limestone knolls where time seems to have stood still since at least 1462, when it was recorded as Denglerene. The Dinkling Green of today deserves a short pause to check the date stones and architectural features on the buildings of this delightful hamlet which occupies the site of a late medieval settlement. House sparrows, swallows and starlings take up residence in the old farm buildings, and nearby kingfishers may be seen on the stream. During October, flocks of fieldfare and redwing often gather in very large numbers in trees and hedgerows in the vicinity and indeed throughout suitable areas of Bowland where there is a good crop of berries.

From Dinkling Green go through a small gate between a garden wall and a farm and cross the field. Go over the stile to the left of the gateway and follow the fence to a footbridge on the right. Cross the bridge to Higher Fence and enter the farmyard. Follow the lane uphill close to limestone knolls and caves to Tungstall Ings, and beyond to the unclassified road linking Burholme Bridge with Chipping. Turn left on the road and look for the footpath sign on the right in order to reach New

A magical sky illuminates the Bowland landscape. *Author's collection.*

*Laund Farm. Leave New Laund and descend to the river Hodder. Cross the step-
ping stones to reach Whitewell.*

Along this walk dry stone walls and barns provide sites for pied wagtails to
conceal their nests. The undulating escarpments of the Hodder Valley and
the limestone knolls provide more suitable habitat for buzzards, which may
be seen rising on thermals and announcing themselves with a distinctive
mewing call. This raptor will be likely focused on the next meal of small
mammal, bird or even carrion – whatever takes its fancy on that day's menu!
If finishing the walk towards the end of the day in early spring there may be
greater opportunities to savour the atmosphere of the natural world, so why
not time your walk accordingly?

At dusk a solitary vocal robin delivers its melancholy, rusty and
somewhat monotonous song cycle, and a roding woodcock, silhouetted
just above the tree line, patrols territorially across the wooded Whitewell
Gorge. The overall atmosphere might be enriched by a tawny owl giving its
well-known hoot or perhaps even the spooky outline of a white barn owl
in pursuit of its prey – usually a selection of voles, shrews, wood mouse,
perhaps a bird or two and other gastronomic delights. The night shift also
features noctule bats flying over the riverine woodlands, while Daubenton's
bats skim the surface of the Hodder. Pipistrelle and long-eared bats are
more likely to be found in closer association with man, around the church
and the inn. In fact, a single pipistrelle will enjoy the local cuisine of up to
3,000 midges in one night.

If you are also in need of refreshments, then you may choose to visit the
Inn at Whitewell. Perfect sobriety will ensure that you do not see any cave
dwellers or fairies either, although there is evidence that cave dwellers lived
in this area around 1000 BC. Within recent times Bronze Age archaeological
finds have been made in the 'Fairy Caves' above the Whitewell Gorge and
indeed in the river itself. A Bronze Age stone used for the grinding of grain
was found in the Hodder in 1984 by Mr Bowman of the Inn at Whitewell and
has been dubbed 'The Whitewell Stone'. So stay sober and happy birding!

Opposite The Inn at Whitewell. *Courtesy of Malcolm Greenhalgh.*

Abbeystead & the two River Wyres

Start/finish	Start and finish at the informal car park near Stoops Bridge, Abbeystead
Grid Ref	SD564544
Distance	6.5 miles (10.5 kilometres)
Time	5 hours
Grade	Easy to moderate
General	Public toilets and refreshment facilities at Dunsop Bridge

This walk is a circular extension of the Wyre Way, going outward to the Tarnbrook Wyre and returning via the Marshaw Wyre. Follow the Wyre Way logo and Ordnance Survey Outdoor Leisure 41 map. Walk east from Stoops Bridge at Abbeystead leaving the main road at a bungalow (right) at the top of the hill. Follow the Wyre Way logo and yellow waymarkers across fields, keeping right of Higher Emmetts Farm and crossing the main road to arrive at 'Top of Emmetts'. Keep right of the building, following the line of the hedge to reach a cluster of three stiles. Veer left across a field heading towards a prominent barn and passing (right) alongside it. Follow a hedge (right) crossing several stiles, and the Tarnbrook Wyre to arrive at the hamlet of Tarnbrook.

This is another great scenic walk, embracing a diversity of countryside within Bowland. The perfect introduction to the area is the popular tourist road route through the Trough of Bowland. This walk incorporates a section of the pass that cuts through the high fells of central Bowland, alongside ancient stands of Scots pines, before the road crosses the old boundary between Lancashire and Yorkshire at 'Boundary Hill'. Contrary to popular belief the Trough of Bowland is not the whole of Bowland; it is in fact the scenic section of the road which extends from Sykes to Marshaw. A Roman road bisects land that was once the haunt of wolves, evidenced by names like 'Wolf Fell' and 'Wolfenhall'.

Opposite Always worth a second look – the little owl is the smallest member of the owl family. *Courtesy of Peter Smith.*

Spotted flycatcher – an appropriately named though declining species.
Courtesy of Peter Smith.

This route provides an opportunity to spot several of Bowland's characteristic birds and the period late April to early May is recommended as the best time to do the walk, which follows the attractive riverine habitats of the two river Wyres, a traditional haunt of dipper, common sandpiper and grey wagtail. Tracing the actual source of the Wyre is not for the faint-hearted because the two tributaries that form the main river originate high on the fells of Tarnbrook and Marshaw Fell respectively, before reaching the confluence at Abbeystead. We will not be going to these sources, so conserve your energy and just enjoy the birdwatching in a spectacular historic landscape. Many species occur in the woodlands and open country along the route from Abbeystead and the remote hamlet of Tarnbrook, including song and mistle thrush, finch, titmice, robin, wren, reed bunting, pied and grey wagtails, jackdaw and the inevitable pheasant. Resident ravens are often seen or heard croaking high above, having extended their range into Bowland from the Lake District. Look out for the stock dove which frequents several of the farm buildings, and in summer, swallow and swift.

One of the first signs of spring is the bubbling note of the curlew's repertoire that is both evocative and haunting, as it returns from the coast to traditional upland breeding grounds. In upland pasture and in-bye between March and July, curlew, snipe, lapwing, redshank and oystercatcher fill the Bowland landscape with their vocal tones and visual displays. The habitat hereabouts is one of the best for breeding waders, and indeed Bowland's breeding lapwing and curlew population is one of the most significant in England. During the season both species may be seen performing their aerial displays while courageously mobbing any intruders such as crows and raptors. Between October and December mixed flocks of fieldfare and redwing are commonly seen, often in large numbers before Christmas, and these roving flocks are likely to turn up almost anywhere, including flying over the fells.

At Tarnbrook turn right along the track and where it divides, take the right fork, turning left over a footbridge preceding farm buildings. On reaching two barns take the right-hand gate and head up Speight Clough, passing a plantation (left) and gate/stile, proceeding onto open moorland near Greenside. At this point use binoculars to reveal well-hidden yellow waymarkers and the location of equally obscure wall stiles. Cross over the moor broadly south-east on a left diagonal, heading towards a substantial track bearing a fingerpost above Tower Lodge.

Turn right on the track to Tower Lodge and right again along the main road for approximately two miles. Carry straight on past a road junction (left) and shortly thereafter regain the Wyre Way footpath. Follow the yellow waymarkers back to Stoops Bridge, crossing over several footbridges straddling the Marshaw Wyre. After climbing up some stone steps, gain a good view of Abbeystead Mansion, the country seat of the Duke of Westminster.

After discovering the hamlet of Tarnbrook we again cross the Tarnbrook Wyre where the route ascends to higher ground. Here flocks of introduced red-legged partridge abound and perky spring wheatear feed in the fields and nest in the walls. Both redstart and pied wagtail also use holes for nesting. Despite the redstart's superb colouration it can be elusive, but in spring the singing male may be located by the rather feeble whirring song delivered from high up in dense foliage in upland plantations such as that at 'Harry Wood'. Watch out for stonechat that has expanded its range into the upland areas of Bowland and is now more frequently observed in heather and tall bracken than its close relative the increasingly uncommon whinchat. The cuckoo and ring ousel also seem to be rapidly gaining the dubious status of 'uncommon' in many former haunts, although on this walk it may be possible to hear a cuckoo or observe a ring ousel moving to higher ground in early spring. The plight of diminishing summer migrants to Britain, such as the cuckoo, spotted flycatcher, yellow wagtail, tree pipit, whinchat and ring ousel is alarming. It is suspected that there are a number of factors contributing to this, including, for example, changes in agricultural practice in Third World countries or the indiscriminate shooting and trapping of millions of birds in Mediterranean countries such as Malta and Cyprus.

Close to Tower Lodge in the Trough of Bowland we gain the Marshaw Wyre, where there is a wonderful stand of Scots pine, which attracts flocks of crossbill and other coniferous-loving species such as goldcrest, coal tit, siskin and lesser redpoll. During 'crossbill invasions' the cone-bearing trees support noisy flocks – winter and early spring are the best times to look for the distinctive red males and green females with their intriguing crossed lower and upper mandible. The Trough road at Marshaw is a good vantage point from which to watch for red grouse that are commonly seen in the heather areas but never in the lowlands of England. Management of

A male whinchat is yet another of Bowland's rather special birds. *Courtesy of Peter Smith.*

The Langden Valley in the heart of Bowland. *Author's collection.*

the grouse moors for shooting has preserved the predominantly heather-covered landscape which is crucial for a variety of birds that rely on this habitat, including hen harrier, short-eared owl and merlin. Sightings of red kite are increasing throughout the Bowland area as a result of successful introduction schemes elsewhere in Britain. Scanning the heather moorland areas for raptors usually produces the best results in spring and may reveal a handsome male hen harrier, quartering the heather or indulging in a display known as 'skydancing', while making a food-pass to the contrasting brown-coloured female. Unfortunately, this characteristic though often maltreated bird of prey, which is indeed the emblem of the Forest of Bowland, did not nest during 2012 – consequently the future does not augur well for this stunning species. The much smaller merlin uses its superb turn of speed to fly down its main prey, the meadow pipit. Peregrines are now quite well established in the Forest of Bowland and in late spring families can be seen together in the sky, giving superb, vocal aerial displays. Hunting peregrines are masters of the sky, renowned for attacking prey from above at speeds of around 200 miles per hour. This is also prime habitat for the diurnal hunting short-eared owl, whose population fluctuates, the greatest numbers occurring in years when voles are abundant. The distinctive shape and rounded wings of a sparrowhawk may also be glimpsed flying across the open fell, before disappearing into a plantation while in pursuit of small birds. By contrast, the kestrel or windhover provides more opportunity for observation as it hovers over the fell with eyes focused on small mammalian prey.

Descending along the wooded valley of the Marshaw Wyre, look and listen for pied and spotted flycatchers, redstart and warbler. The distinctive songs of blackcap, garden warbler, chiffchaff and willow warbler help to locate them singing from trees and woodland scrub.

This account has mainly alluded to birding in Bowland during early spring, but in winter you can enjoy an equally nice walk, especially when the weather is crisp and bright. Although the bird scene may be quieter in other seasons there will always be something to watch, not least the superb changing landscapes.